# Halcyon Days

# Halcyon Days

An American Family through
Three Generations

*Peggie Phipps Boegner*

*and Richard Gachot*

Old Westbury Gardens and
Harry N. Abrams, Inc.,
Publishers, New York

Dedicated to my three Ditas—P.P.B.

*Acknowledgments*

During the long, often arduous course of this
project, we were greatly helped by the contributions of many people and would like to thank
them all, especially Barbara Burn, Martina D'Alton,
Gwen Mackay, James Mills, Virginia Prince, and
Michael Shroyer, and with a special thank you to
Marjorie Buddington for her unflagging enthusiasm in assisting with Part II, Memories.

© 1986 by Peggie Phipps Boegner and Richard Gachot
All rights reserved

Library of Congress Cataloging-in-Publication Data
Boegner, Peggie Phipps, 1906–
    Halcyon days.
    1. Phipps family. 2. United States—Biography.
3. Phipps family—Pictorial works. I. Gachot, Richard.
II. Title.
CT274.P53B64   1986   929'.2'0973   86-8460
ISBN 0-8109-1064-0

Old Westbury Gardens, Inc.
Old Westbury, New York 11568

Photographic editing by Richard Gachot
Designed by Michael Shroyer
Edited by Martina D'Alton
Printed in Japan

False title page: *John H. H. ("Ben") Phipps, 1904*
Frontispiece: from left, *Michael Phipps, Lillias Kent, and
Peggie, Ben, and Barbara Phipps in their costumes for*
Midsummer Night's Dream, *1914*

# Genealogy

## THE PHIPPS FAMILY

Henry Phipps, Jr.
(1839–1934)
m. Annie C. Shaffer
(1850–1959)

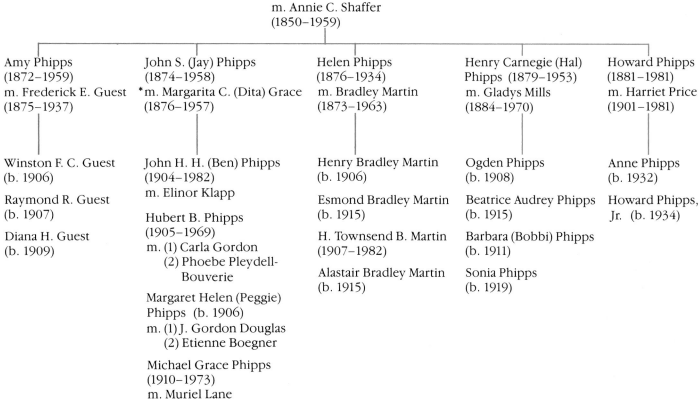

Amy Phipps
(1872–1959)
m. Frederick E. Guest
(1875–1937)

Winston F. C. Guest
(b. 1906)

Raymond R. Guest
(b. 1907)

Diana H. Guest
(b. 1909)

John S. (Jay) Phipps
(1874–1958)
*m. Margarita C. (Dita) Grace
(1876–1957)

John H. H. (Ben) Phipps
(1904–1982)
m. Elinor Klapp

Hubert B. Phipps
(1905–1969)
m. (1) Carla Gordon
    (2) Phoebe Pleydell-
      Bouverie

Margaret Helen (Peggie)
Phipps (b. 1906)
m. (1) J. Gordon Douglas
    (2) Etienne Boegner

Michael Grace Phipps
(1910–1973)
m. Muriel Lane

Helen Phipps
(1876–1934)
m. Bradley Martin
(1873–1963)

Henry Bradley Martin
(b. 1906)

Esmond Bradley Martin
(b. 1915)

H. Townsend B. Martin
(1907–1982)

Alastair Bradley Martin
(b. 1915)

Henry Carnegie (Hal)
Phipps (1879–1953)
m. Gladys Mills
(1884–1970)

Ogden Phipps
(b. 1908)

Beatrice Audrey Phipps
(b. 1915)

Barbara (Bobbi) Phipps
(b. 1911)

Sonia Phipps
(b. 1919)

Howard Phipps
(1881–1981)
m. Harriet Price
(1901–1981)

Anne Phipps
(b. 1932)

Howard Phipps,
Jr. (b. 1934)

## THE GRACE FAMILY

Michael Paul (Grandpoods) Grace
(1842–1920)
m. Margarita A. (Grandmoods) Mason

Elisa Grace
(1872–?)
m. Hubert Beaumont

Michael Beaumont
(b. 1903)

Elena Grace
(1874–?)
m. Viscount Suirdale,
Lord Donoughmore

John Michael (Ordy) Suirdale
(b. 1903)

Doreen Hely-Hutchinson
(b. 1906)

David Hely-Hutchinson
(b. 1911)

*Margarita C. (Dita) Grace
(1876–1957)

Gladys Grace
(1888–1978)
m. (1) Raymond Hamilton-Grace
    (2) Joseph (Josh) Benskin

Anne Grace
(b. 1914)

*Margarita Phipps with three of her children,* from left, *Peggie, Hubert, and Ben at Battle Abbey, England, 1906*

# CONTENTS

*Margarita Grace, 1894, dressed for her presentation to the Court of Queen Victoria*

# PREFACE

A few years ago I started writing down the memories of my life in Westbury House. This was partly for fun and partly to leave the history of our family to my grandchildren. It was also, and perhaps primarily, to provide a true background for the visitors who came to see the Old Westbury Gardens. Most of the public seemed to take such a genuine and kindly interest in anything to do with the house and the family.

At the same time, but separately, Dick Gachot, my friend and next door neighbor, was doing architectural research on Westbury House. In a closet on the third floor he found several boxes of my grandfather's letters. Grandpa always avoided publicity so the few lines that have been written about him have only appeared briefly in the biographies of Mr. Carnegie and Mr. Frick. These new-found letters that have never been seen cast a fascinating light on both his family and business affairs. As his letters are so straightforward and good I don't think he would have minded some of them being printed.

In several trunks Dick found an even greater cache of over two thousand marvelous old family photographs dating from 1865 to 1930. It took him two years to sort and restore them.

In 1983, we decided that we would put together the photographs, letters, and my memories to create a book that would faithfully portray the gracious way of life that existed here during the early part of the century.

Peggie Phipps Boegner

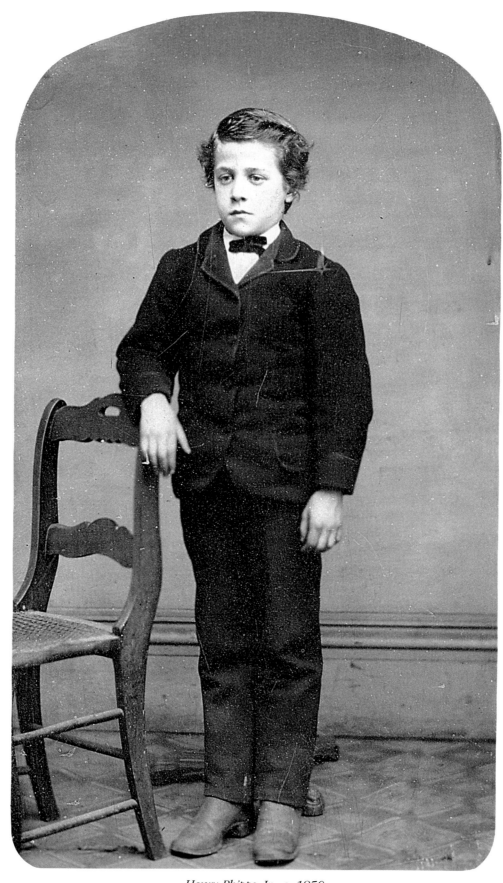

*Henry Phipps, Jr., c. 1850*

# I. Beginnings

Five years ago while doing restoration work for Old Westbury Gardens, I came across three steamer trunks in a far off corner of the attic of Westbury House. They had been there untouched for over sixty years. Inside were more than three thousand of Henry Phipps' personal letters, family photographs, and other correspondence, dating from 1860 to 1920. One trunk contained nothing but photographs— stacks of neatly piled daguerrotypes, tintypes, cartes de visite, glass plates, portraits, and snapshots. As a devotee of early photography, I was quick to realize the span of history that lay before me on film, if only the people and places could be identified. The other trunks of letters, diaries, and memorabilia, dating from the same period, held the answers, and so began my years of research and photographic restoration that eventually culminated in this book.

The documents found in the trunks traced Henry Phipps' meteoric rise from cobbler's son to millionaire steelmaster and philanthropist. As Andrew Carnegie's partner and the second largest stockholder in Carnegie Steel, Phipps possessed a financial genius which is largely a matter of record, but little is known or has been written of his personal life to date. Shy and retiring by nature, he shunned all publicity attendant upon the other great industrialists of his age and remained by choice a private person. He paid for this privacy by being often misunderstood while alive and all but forgotten after his death.

The newly discovered letters, which comprise much of Part I, provide an honest insight into the personal life of one of our nation's early industrial giants. They reveal the strengths and frailties of a self-made man's iron work ethic and the anxieties that he and his wife felt, especially in raising their five children, while adapting to the new socio-economic changes that they daily faced. Restrained by their background of poverty and strict Victorian morality, Phipps and his wife managed to meet, though never fully enjoy, the social presentment demanded of them by this new lifestyle.

Another trunk in the attic of Westbury House contained letters from the Phipps children to their parents, and many of these are quoted herein. I have taken the liberty of correcting most spelling mistakes but have largely let the letters stand on their own, reflecting the styles and personalities of the writers. The children's letters illuminate the early lives of a second generation who, born into a more privileged lifestyle, were comfortable within the upper echelons of society in a manner unknown to their parents. That Henry Phipps could have told his eldest son Jay, the focus here of the second generation, "Don't play polo or buy polo ponies—that's only for the rich . . . you can't afford it," reflects his own morality more than fact, for when he said these words he was a millionaire many times over. That Jay went on to own the best string of ponies on Long Island while at the same time administering his affairs with his father's thrift reveals the inescapable influence of each passing generation on the next.

It was to be the third generation who would most fully enjoy the world that father and grandfather had created for them. This world is seen through the eyes of Jay's daughter Peggie whose childhood memories of life in Westbury House in its early days are collected in Part II. They provide an unusual opportunity to view the day-to-day life of a child in a rarefied world of the past; it is very much a view from within rather than outside that world.

Though the book spans the lifetime of three generations of the Phipps family, it is not intended to be a comprehensive family biography or history of the time. It is simply a collection of unpublished personal letters, written memories, and extraordinary photographs, which through juxtaposition of words and pictures portrays the contrasting lifestyles of these three generations. It encompasses a memorable hundred years of our country's history that began as a dream of "rags to riches" in 1850, evolved into the gracious way of life of the early 1900s, and all but ended by 1950.

Richard Gachot

*The Philadelphia birthplace of Henry Phipps, Jr., as it appeared around 1850*

# HENRY PHIPPS, JR.

Steel. In post-Civil War America, steel and the raw materials wrested from the earth fueled the new industrial age. Out of steel came the railroads, bridges, and skyscrapers, and the fortunes that could turn a poor cobbler's son into one of the wealthiest men in America.

Henry Phipps, Jr., called Harry for most of his life, was born in Philadelphia on September 27, 1839, the third child of Henry, Sr., and Hannah Frank Phipps, emigrants from Shropshire, England. Henry, Sr., was a cobbler, earning his living by selling shoes from the back of a horse-drawn cart. In 1845, Henry and Hannah decided to move with their four children—John, William, Harry, and Amelia—to Allegheny City (now part of Pittsburgh) where they settled in an area known as Barefoot Square. Their neighbors on Rebecca Street were William and Margaret Carnegie and their sons, Andrew and Tom.

Living next door to each other, the two families developed close ties. In his autobiography, Andrew Carnegie wrote that his mother "earned four dollars a week binding shoes" made by Phipps, Sr., and he himself became a fast friend of John Phipps. As they grew up the two young men formed part of the nucleus of a group that met regularly in the back room of Phipps' cobbler's shop to debate the issues of the day and to dream about the future. Young Henry had also formed a close friendship with Andrew's younger brother, Tom. Referring to this in his autobiography, Andrew recalled that "as children they played together, and throughout life, until my brother's death in 1886, these two formed, as it were, a partnership within a partnership. . . . What one did the other did."[1]

It was a hard life on Barefoot Square, and the three Phipps brothers determined early to escape its poverty and to avoid "the confinement incident to the cobbler's bench. I hope it will not be my lot," wrote John in 1857, "ever to resume the family trade. Once free from its shackles, it would be hard to put on the chains again." By then, one brother had already escaped; William had become a Methodist minister, or, as John wrote, "quitted the bench for the Pulpit

*Henry Phipps, Jr. — "Harry" — c. 1857*

and rather than working on soles was working for Souls." John too would never return to the bench, for soon afterward, he was tragically killed in a fall from a horse.

Harry attended the public schools of Allegheny until the age of fourteen, and as his brothers had done before him, he assisted his father at the despised cobbler's bench. After leaving school, he worked for the next three years as an apprentice in a jeweler's shop, earning $1.25 a week. Decades later, Harry recalled this time in a letter to his own son, Jay:

> I went to the office before seven in the morning. In the Winter rose in the dark in an unwarmed house, in a room where the water often froze in the pitcher. . . . A long day's duties found

---

1. Andrew Carnegie, *Autobiography of Andrew Carnegie* (Boston: Houghton Mifflin Co., 1924), p. 132.

*Henry Phipps, Sr., c. 1856*

*Harry Phipps in 1861, a partner at Dilworth and Bidwell*

me at home in the evening glad to be with my dear Father & Mother, Brothers & Sister. No thought of pleasure save as it was found in the discharge of duty. Have I ever regretted this self denial, no. Does the husbandman regret the seed he sows?

Harry's apprentice wages were doubled in 1856, but by then he was ready to move up into the business world, inspired perhaps by a letter from his brother John in the spring of that year: "Life was not given to us to be frittered away in dreamy Indolence. There is room enough in this great world for all of us to exercise our talents and energy. So much is there to be learnt, so much work to perform, that I frequently think the span of Existence is scarcely long enough to accomplish it . . . Don't you think the star of the Phipps Family in the ascendant? Who knows what may yet happen to that aspiring race."

John may not have lived to see the dream fulfilled, but following his untimely death, his boyhood friend, Andrew Carnegie, kept a kindly eye on Harry, who, wrote Carnegie in his autobiography, "was several years my junior, but had not failed to attract my attention as a bright, clever lad. One day he asked his brother, John, to lend him a quarter of a dollar. John saw that he had important use for it and handed him the shining quarter without inquiry. Next morning an advertisement appeared in the 'Pittsburgh Dispatch': 'A willing boy wishes work.' This was the use the energetic and willing Harry had made of his quarter, probably the first quarter he had ever spent at one time in his life."[2]

The advertisement brought Harry to the attention of Dilworth and Bidwell, dealers in iron and railroad spikes. He was hired as an errand boy and, as Carnegie put it, "launched himself upon the sea of business. There was no holding back a boy like that."[3]

For five years, Harry also attended night classes in accounting in which he apparently excelled, for, in 1861, at the age of twenty-two, he became the firm's bookkeeper and was offered a partnership. Not long afterward, his reputation as a first-rate bookkeeper reached another Barefoot Square friend, Tom Miller. At Miller's recommendation and with eight hundred dollars loaned to him by Miller, Harry became a partner, in Kloman Brothers, an iron works which manufactured railroad equipment. Harry held onto his job at Dilworth's, but now, each night, he also walked the three miles to Kloman's to work on their books as well. His star was indeed in the ascendant, and soon Kloman Brothers became Kloman and Phipps.

---

2. Carnegie, *Autobiography,* p. 132.
3. Carnegie, *Autobiography,* p. 132.

*The Phipps brothers, c. 1860:* from left, *Harry, William, and John*

*At Knebworth House, in England, 1892:* from left, *Harry Phipps, Henry Clay Frick, unidentified man, Harry's son Hal, Annie Phipps;* seated, far right, *daughter Helen;* standing, second from right, *daughter Amy*

The company grew and prospered and eventually, in 1865, merged with Miller's and Carnegie's Cyclops Iron Company to form the Union Iron Mills. It was a time of tremendous growth in America. The industrial revolution was well underway, the railroads were creeping westward, and the Civil War had brought great profits to the burgeoning iron industry. The Union Iron Mills expanded apace in all directions and through subsequent mergers, became Carnegie Brothers (1881) and Carnegie, Phipps Company (1886) until both were reorganized as the Carnegie Steel Company (1892) of which Henry Phipps, Jr., the cobbler's son from Barefoot Square, was the second largest stockholder next only to Andrew Carnegie.

Phipps became treasurer of the company because of his extraordinary grasp of finance and accounting procedures; he was a wizard at bookkeeping. Perhaps his impoverished childhood and innate frugality had provided him with the incentive to tackle tedious bookkeeping with the same zeal as a child playing a favorite game, for he often worked sixteen hours a day without complaint. He carefully scrutinized all

matters of credit, loans, discounts, and payroll to assure the highest return on each dollar that passed through his hands. He became a master at "floating" the dollar to the company's advantage when cash was scarce. During these years, a story was told about Harry making the rounds of the banks along Wood Street daily in a carriage drawn by his black mare, Gypsy. The old horse was so accustomed to the route that she needed no directions from Harry. She moved diagonally, back and forth, from one side of the street to the other, from bank to bank, waiting patiently outside each stop until Harry had completed his business. So ingrained was the routine, that it was said to be impossible to induce Gypsy to follow a straight line down the street.

Even when loans were due, Harry often used his wizardry at juggling figures to persuade the banks that it would be to their advantage to waive payment for a few more days, thus providing the capital needed for the rapid expansion of the Carnegie steel empire. Phipps' ability to make the same dollar do many jobs was his special genius. It was said that "no one could keep a check longer in the air without funds to meet it" than Harry Phipps.[4]

Harry could apply the same sense of thrift to the manufacturing end of the business and on two occasions actually turned waste into profits. Flue cinder, a by-product of the blast furnace, lay in great piles outside the iron mills on the banks of the Monongahela River. Phipps found that this "waste" product could be substituted for the puddle cinder which was necessary in the manufacture of mill-iron. In fact, it was better because it had a lower phosphorus content than puddle cinder, meaning that instead of 80 percent iron ore to 20 percent puddle cinder, the Carnegie firm could produce high quality mill-iron with only 40 percent of the costly ore to 60 percent flue cinder. Phipps' other contribution was made in the steel-rolling mill. He discovered that "scale" ( the chips and shavings thrown off as the hot metal passed through the rollers) could be reheated and rolled into high-grade steel. Until then it had simply been swept out of the mill as waste at the end of each day. Thanks to Phipps' sense of thrift and his ingenuity, the Carnegie firm not only saved tremendous amounts by recycling its own flue cinder and scale but was able to buy these waste products for very little from the other firms along the river before the competition knew what was happening.

In 1886, after the death of Tom Carnegie, Phipps was made chairman of Carnegie Brothers. It was understood that this was a temporary assignment, until the right man could be found for the job, and three years later, such a man came along—Henry Clay Frick. The Frick Coke Works had become aligned with Carnegie Brothers in 1881, and over the ensuing years, Andrew Carnegie had been favorably impressed with Frick's managerial talents. Under Frick's new leadership, the various Carnegie Steel interests were restructured into a unified whole; from mining the ore to rolling the steel, every aspect of the steel-making business was performed by the company, and all profits were paid into its coffers.

However, despite Frick's contributions, his presence in the Carnegie firm was always an uneasy one, and there were several sharp differences of opinion between chairman Frick and the controlling stockholder, Carnegie, which were eventually to become irreconcilable. As early as 1894, Phipps could see the storm brewing, and to his son Jay, he wrote, "This Christmas to me has been marked by a series of serious cables from A.C. [Andrew Carnegie] in regard to the Chm leaving us; of course it is the egotism & bad temper of the one who is not unknown for his

Andrew Carnegie, c. 1884

exhibitions. It looked on the 21st as tho I must at once go home, and the strain has more or less continued until this morning when a cable from Mr. F said 'Everything arranged satisfactorily.' It seems A.C. must have climbed down a very long and steep way; in fact I went so far as to cable that unless something was done, I intimated I wished to retire. A.C. was awful hot at H.C.F. who was the wronged one & had my sympathies & best support."

On such occasions when the amicable relationship between Phipps and Carnegie could have been strained by open conflict over business matters, a silent understanding, born of years of mutual respect, enabled them to transcend their differences. With a simple exchange of words, using the private language of a lifetime friendship, Phipps wrote to Carnegie, "Troubles unnumbered—unending, life too short, the game not worth the candle. When fair times come again, an arrangement can be made whereby we can have a haven of enjoyment and rest, instead of what may beset us any day, a sea of trouble, cares, anxieties."[5]

Carnegie accepted the philosophical words of his "old pard" with the wisdom of give-and-take by which each had prospered over the years. Soon afterward,

4. Joseph Frazier Wall, *Andrew Carnegie* (New York: Oxford University Press, 1970), p. 252.

5. Louis M. Hacker, *The World of Andrew Carnegie* (Philadelphia: J. B. Lippincott Co., 1968), p. 414.

*A gathering at Knebworth House, c. 1895:* standing, third from left, *Harry Phipps;* seated, far right, *Andrew Carnegie*

Harry reflected on that friendship, again in a letter to his son Jay: "Spent some hours last Saturday pleasantly with Mr. AC, walking and talking. He is an unusually interesting, conscientious and bright man, and in many [more] ways than money I am indebted to my association with him."

In 1899, however, when the storm that hung over the Frick-Carnegie relationship finally broke in public, Phipps was again on Frick's side. The confrontation began with a disagreement over Carnegie fixing the price of the coke that the Frick Coke Works sold to Carnegie Steel, and it came to a head when an enraged Carnegie urged the board to pass a resolution calling for Frick to resign and return to them his interest in Carnegie Steel at book value, under the terms of the company's so-called Ironclad Agreement of 1887. Book value was far below the real value of the shares as all the partners well knew, and Frick filed an equity suit against Carnegie Steel that rocked the industrial world and drew headline publicity in the international press.

Over the years, Harry had remained the quiet partner, aloof from the many company quarrels between the vociferous Carnegie and his other partners.

Now, for the first time, Harry was compelled to break their silent understanding and to challenge his old pard openly. While the other major partners in the company, recognizing Carnegie's control over their future, bowed to his wishes and signed the resolution regardless of their personal feelings, Phipps withheld his signature. He had always scrupulously maintained his full independence in thought and action. He believed Carnegie guilty of wrongfully exploiting a moral principle dear to him in the handling of the Frick matter. However, to avoid head-on conflict with his old friend, he tempered his objections to Carnegie's demands by reminding him that he "would do pretty much as you would wish, as it always gives me pleasure to concur with you—when I can properly do so. A right decision in this matter is less important to me in its effects upon my pocket than its influence upon my mind. To feel that I have been rightly treated is a greater pleasure to me than any probable or possible gain in money; that is subordinate, the first is everything; and next to it is the feeling that the business in which my heart has ever been, has been dealt with on time honored, safe and just business principles."

Some years later, George Harvey, a contemporary of the principals, captured the mood of this confrontation between Phipps and Carnegie; he described Phipps as a well-cast peacemaker, who alone

> could meet [Carnegie] on the same level; the two had toiled shoulder to shoulder as partners for nearly forty years and had shared a prosperity far surpassing any registered in the dreams of either; each admired and respected the other; between them was no jealousy; their friendship had never been seriously shaken; they were growing old. . . . They were still "Harry" and "Andrew" to each other, but for how long? Appearances had been safeguarded scrupulously. Mr. Carnegie had shown, perhaps had felt, no resentment at what he must have considered a personal defection, and Mr. Phipps had confined the protest which he felt bound to make to the smallest formal compass. The public detected no more than a difference in judgment; their associates, with minds possessed by self-interest, prudently perceived nothing. But the two concerned knew that at last a rift was opening which must be closed quickly or it would widen beyond possibility of repair. The one must have been as surely conscious as the other was clearly aware of the entrance into their relationship of the fatal element of mistrust.[6]

Harry Phipps, at age sixty, nearing retirement, had placed his net worth as a partner and friend on the line over a simple matter of principle. Carnegie, aged sixty-four, accustomed to having things his own way and just as unbending in matters of personal principle, listened to Harry's words and responded simply, "Make your own plan, Harry, I only want what is fair."

The conflict with Frick was settled out of court in 1900, when both men agreed to a reorganization of the two companies; Carnegie Steel and the Frick Coke Works became separate divisions of the new Carnegie Company with a combined capitalization of $320 million, a far more realistic figure than the $25 million Carnegie had wanted to use as a basis for buying out Frick's share. Carnegie and Phipps both wanted to retire, while Frick, no longer an active participant in the company, was not pleased with the inactivity and also wanted out. The stage was set for the sale of the new Carnegie Company to J. P. Morgan's United States Steel Corporation. However, Andrew and Harry, the old ironmasters, could not sit idle the last year of their company's existence. Instead, with

6. George Harvey, *Henry Clay Frick: The Man* (New York: Charles Scribner's Sons, 1928), p. 250–51.

renewed energy, they earned in 1900 their largest profit ever ($40 million) which allowed them to push the selling price of the Carnegie Company up to $480 million, of which Carnegie's share was $226 million and Phipps' $40 million.

After the sale of the company, Frick and Carnegie never again spoke to each other, but Phipps and Carnegie remained "Harry" and "Andrew" to each other, friends to the end. Both men retired to that "haven of enjoyment and rest," spending their remaining years with their families and their philanthropies.

In the 1880s, Phipps had begun making donations, sometimes sizable, but "only to causes he believed just," and his earliest gifts had created quite a storm, making Pittsburgh newspaper headlines. In donating $25,000 to the Pittsburgh Library, and in making larger donations to the city for public parks, playgrounds, reading rooms, baths, and a conservatory, Phipps had stipulated that all these places be kept open on Sunday. The city's ministry was outraged, denouncing him for desecrating the traditions of the "Lord's Day" and creating a "public nuisance." Even in the face of such disapproval, the city finally bowed to public opinion and accepted the gifts with the stipulation attached.

On May 3, 1886, thousands of grateful beneficiaries of Phipps' generosity gathered in the street outside his home to honor him with a concert and serenade by local German singing societies. The last thing Harry had wanted was more public controversy or this demonstration, but after a few hours of thoroughly enjoying the singing, he finally stepped forward to recognize the tribute and spoke:

> As you were playing I thought to myself that such delightful music ought to be heard even on Sunday by the poor people who cannot hear it on other days. . . . I take it that this outpouring is not really a compliment to your humble servant, but is expressive of the growing sentiment of our people that the public libraries, as well as parks, greenhouses and other places of this kind be opened on Sunday, in order to make life bright and cheerful to those who work so hard other days. . . . In my childhood days I knew what a strict Sunday meant. My parents were so strict that they thought it a sin to even walk on Sunday or indulge in any innocent recreation. . . . I thank you sincerely, dear friends, for this compliment, and I hope the good work of establishing a liberal Sunday will progress wisely and with speed.

The early Pittsburgh gifts were the smallest of Harry's philanthropies, but they are most revealing of his strong convictions. Believing that health was not

*On a heathered moor in Scotland, c. 1888:* foreground from left, *Harry Phipps, his daughter Amy and wife Annie;* background, third, fourth, and fifth from left, *Harry's daughter Helen with Andrew and Louise Carnegie*

only essential but inseparable from man's well-being, Phipps was greatly concerned with the prevention and treatment of tuberculosis. In 1903, the Henry Phipps Institute for the Study, Treatment and Prevention of Tuberculosis was opened at the University of Pennsylvania. By 1919, his gifts to it had totaled $3 million, and the institute became a permanent part of the university. In 1905, he also founded the Phipps Tuberculosis Dispensary at Johns Hopkins Hospital in Baltimore, and when, in 1909, the Pennsylvania State Legislature rejected a plan to underwrite the cost of beds in state hospitals that were used for tuberculosis patients, Phipps personally assumed this financial burden.

Hand in hand with health went housing. Having been raised in a poor neighborhood, Harry was well aware of the demoralizing effects of poverty. Sensitive to the need for better living conditions and housing for city dwellers, in 1905, he announced his plans to build "Phipps Houses" for middle- and low-income tenants. The Phipps buildings were designed to have ample light and air, to be fireproof and sanitary, and to provide space for children to play. In 1906, the first Phipps Houses were built at 325–35 East 31st

Street in Manhattan, designed by architect Grosvenor Atterbury. These 142-family buildings became the model for housing authorities in New York and other cities.

Phipps' other philanthropies ranged far and wide, large and small—$350,000 for relief of Boer War widows and orphans; $150,000 in 1910 to establish the Phipps Psychiatric Clinic at Johns Hopkins, with another $1 million in 1924; $100,000 to start an agricultural college in Pusa, India; and $10,000 to Maria Montessori to help her open a school in Rome.

After retirement, Harry gave more than $7 million toward scientific enlightenment. He gave only when and where his heart and mind told him the cause was just. Unlike Carnegie, Harry shunned all publicity about his personal life and philanthropies. The press did not take kindly to this indifference on his part, and articles still appeared in newspapers wherever he traveled, such as this 1906, front-page account of his visit to Denver to see his nephew, Senator Lawrence Phipps:

Henry Phipps, the ironmaster, who has risen from office boy in a spike factory, to the top of the ladder in the steel business of the United States, is in the city today. Nervous, short, thin, anxious to be doing something, Mr. Phipps rose at 6:30 o'clock this morning, and before the members of his party were out of bed had taken his breakfast.

Wearing a short beard, a stiff hat that looks some years out of date, above gray hair cut long in the back, and with a hasty step, accentuated by the pounding of a small cane on the sidewalk, Mr. Phipps' appearance is striking. . . . His trousers are a little short and do not appear to have been cut very well. A long-tailed coat, worn perhaps to make him appear taller, and a dark overcoat of light weight material, which he buttons tightly about him when out of doors, do not appear to be of great value.

*Harry Phipps in his philanthropist years*

But these things bring out the fact more clearly that he is a character above the ordinary. Mr. Phipps refused to be interviewed, but was gentle in his refusal and exhibited politeness that is often lacking in men of wealth.

"Now, now, sir," said Mr. Phipps this morning, "I never permit myself to be interviewed; I am here on a pleasure trip. There is nothing significant in my visit. Really, while I am very fond of newspapermen, I never give out an interview. There are lots of persons whose tongues are longer than their heads, and they will give you plenty to write about, but I don't know a single thing that will interest you."

With his own family and friends, Harry was open and generous; his largess was spontaneous, and because it was neither expected nor asked for, it was all the more meaningful. Among his papers were found many letters from grateful relatives, including this one from his sister Amelia's child, written in 1906:

> Dear Uncle Henry,
> There never was such an uncle as ours! You and Aunt Annie and the girls have taken me to Europe three times and given me the best times I have ever had and now you crown it all with this wonderful present—more than we might earn ourselves by working hard every year. You certainly have made us share in your "jubilee" in a way that we shall remember as long as we live. If you could hear our rejoicings and many plans you would realize how much we appreciate your goodness to us. I wish I could thank you properly dear Uncle but I really don't know how. The gift is so big and our thanks so little. It is all so one-sided. We can only love you and be proud that one of the best as well as most successful men in America is our uncle. It would have made your Brother John happy to know that it was his "little acorn" with which you started.
> With love to all I am ever your affectionate and grateful niece,
> Janet C. Walker

The "little acorn" she mentions was the quarter John had given Harry to pay for his advertisement, "A willing boy wishes work," nearly a lifetime earlier.

*Annie C. Shaffer, 1870*

# ANNIE

In 1872, at age thirty-three, Harry Phipps married Annie Childs Shaffer, a beautiful young woman of German-French descent, eleven years his junior. The Shaffer family was a close one; their Murry Hill house in Allegheny was home not only to the immediate family—Annie's parents John and Margaret, her sister Addie, and brothers Harvey and Wallie—but also to her aunts Sadie and Sophie. Even after Annie's marriage and move to a home of her own, family ties remained strong. Almost every day, letters were exchanged between Annie and the Shaffers, relaying the news or simply reassuring that all was well.

As a young bride coming from such a family-oriented home, Annie Shaffer struggled to make the transition to Mrs. Henry Phipps, Jr., wife of one of Pittsburgh's rising stars of industry. While Harry had his business contacts to smooth his entry into this new world, Annie had only her family and Christian faith to guide her. Twenty-two years old, she had been thrust into an unfamiliar and rapidly changing new life that confused her. While Harry was away on business trips in the early days of their marriage, Annie stayed in Allegheny to care for her aging parents and to raise her young children. In 1873, after the birth of her first child, Amy, she began a Sunday journal; in it, she often recorded her self-doubts and insecurities as she wrestled with the demands of her new station.

The routine management of a large house, the handling of servants, and the social presence expected of a woman in her position were all foreign to her. Time after time, her kind heart muddled her best intentions to manage the household satisfactorily. Accustomed to doing things for herself, she could not get used to the role of servants in her home. "Now today for instance," she wrote in an 1873 journal entry, "while I was in market, Nellie had to mind Amy and let her dishes stand (Biddy was ironing). When I got home of course I found all the work to be done—Amy to be washed and put to sleep and dinner to get. Fortunately I had made the beds before leaving. After washing Amy I was downstairs most of the time helping to get dinner." She was well aware of her shortcomings, of needing "training so very much," as she confided to her journal in another 1873 entry. "It almost overwhelms me at times when I think of my responsibilities and ignorance. Help! Help! I wonder if there was ever such a doubtful fearful erratic creature as A.C.P."

*Annie C. Shaffer in 1870*

In those early days, she often turned to her religious upbringing for guidance, and on one occasion, reflecting on a Sunday sermon on "keeping in mind that we could keep ourselves unspotted from the world," she was prompted to write, "I make mistakes in so many things. How I do wish I could be kind and

*Annie Shaffer Phipps, c. 1875*

*Harry Phipps in 1875*

gentle and above all charitable to others' faults."

Her Christian fervor, which remained with her over the years and continued after her conversion to Christian Science, was a source of comfort that she could not fully share with her husband. Harry might have been "so very good about going to church with me," wrote Annie, "but I feel I have had very little influence as far as persuading him to become a member." Although Harry did not share this important part of Annie's life and although in her confusion Annie might even forget a meaningful date in his life, as she did one year, writing, "Yesterday was Harry's birthday and I didn't even know it," there can be no question of their devotion to each other. It was because of that devotion that Annie was determined to adapt to her new lifestyle as much for her husband as herself. She pressed herself to try to meet each challenge and to improve herself culturally by reading, learning French, taking singing and painting lessons, and "using the dining room while I am alone more often." All of this she did with Harry's encouragement, but she never let these outside pursuits interfere with the values her upbringing told her were more important.

In her Sunday journal, she reveals the deep inner conflict between her desire to move ahead into her new world and her reluctance to leave behind the old. On one hand, she would write: "I enjoy my French lessons very much, and only wish I could let things about the house worry me less. Read last week, 'Modern Skepticism' in 'Scribner's.' It throws no light upon my perplexities." On the other hand, she confided that "if Harry doesn't care much . . . I will not go to so many amusements. I do feel lonely at the thought of being left at home but do not think it is best to have so much excitement while nursing." She could never forget or abandon what her heart told her was important in life. Her family—her children— consumed her, and though she might make casual note in her journal of dinner companions and social gatherings or record that she "had two music lessons and I am going to try and be a good performer," she wrote endlessly about her children's health, detailing, for example, the appearance of new teeth as though such matters were the most significant events of the week, and for her, they were. The fact that "in a week or so Amy will be ten months old and not a tooth yet" was of far greater concern to Annie than any social engagement.

Two years later, Annie was still blaming her failure to "go out more in the world" and take her place in society on her inability to organize her free time after meeting her family responsibilities. She had an uneasy feeling that she "ought to have a great deal of spare time and have things 'tip top' if I only knew how to manage. . . . I have read very little lately—

not nearly as much as I ought with my opportunities. The papers and weeklies are so easily picked up! However I did read 'Cricket on the Hearth' by Dickens before we went to see Booth play it." Yet having again dutifully reported the progress of her social education, she turned quickly to where her heart really was: "Amy grows in mind and body. She talks quite plainly now and has her twenty teeth. The last two are just peeping out. Dear Amy, I would like to kiss her just now."

With the birth of her second child, John (called Jay), in 1874, Annie's efforts at organization began to succeed. On Amy's second birthday, with Jay "sitting up in bed waiting for me, and Amy . . . sound asleep in her crib," she wrote that "housekeeping gets easier and I seem to have more time now than I had when we only had Amy."

In those early years, Annie also seemed to have great difficulty comprehending her husband's wealth, and she worried about her handling of household finances: "Amy is going into flannel dresses. I wish I knew more about dressmaking. . . . Harry promises me a sewing machine." A few months later, he apparently had kept that promise for she wrote: "I have now a dress sewing machine and am going to learn how to use it next week. I got a very good one as it is a thing to last a lifetime." By this time, Harry could easily have bought his wife an entire dressmaking factory, but Annie still had to justify, at least to herself, her choice of a "very good" machine.

Annie's journal for the first decade of her marriage paints a touching picture of a young but determined bride and mother. During that time, she gave birth to her five children. Amy and Jay were followed by Helen in 1876, Hal (Henry Carnegie, so named after Andrew Carnegie) in 1879, and Howard in 1881. By then, she was thirty-one years old and had devoted all her energies to raising her children, running the house, looking after her parents and other Allegheny relations, and expanding her horizons through studies and cultural pursuits.

Only in 1884, when Howard was three years old, did she begin to look beyond the garden wall. She started to travel regularly with Harry and to fill her journal with news of these trips and the new acquaintances she had made. At last Annie had gone out in the world. By 1887, her journal had become a virtual travelogue. With Amy fifteen years old, Jay thirteen and away at school, Helen eleven, Hal eight, and Howard six, the family was growing up and ready for the years of travel ahead. Annie too had grown up. Gone were all traces of her earlier introspection, of self-doubt and insecurity. It had taken fifteen years for the "fearful erratic creature" of 1873 to adapt to her husband's "rising star" and become the confident, commanding

From left, *John and Margaret Shaffer, Annie's parents, with her Aunt Sadie, Pittsburgh, c. 1880*

From left, *Harry and Annie Phipps, Margaret Shaffer, Amy and Jay Phipps, the two oldest Phipps children, San Francisco, c. 1882*

*Amy Phipps, c. 1879*

*John Shaffer ("Jay") Phipps, c. 1877*

*Henry Carnegie ("Hal") Phipps, c. 1881*

*Howard Phipps, c. 1883*

From top, *Amy, Helen, and Jay Phipps, c. 1878*

From left, *Hal, Howard, and Jay, c. 1884*

*Visiting Annie's sister Addie and her family:* far right, in hammock, *Annie and Amy Phipps;* in striped shirt, *Helen;* right foreground, *Howard*

*Helen and Jay, c. 1884*

lady, the grande dame her granddaughter Peggie remembers later in this book. Yet even as the matriarch of one of the wealthiest families of early twentieth-century America, whatever riches and worldly friends this position brought her, Annie remained throughout her life true not only to her Allegheny roots but to those innate values her "good heart" told her were important in life. These were the same values her husband held dear. He had not pushed her to better herself culturally for reasons of social presence; he had merely wanted her to become comfortable in their new lifestyle. His concern for Annie's well-being is clearly expressed in a letter to his children in January 1882:

> My Dear Children,
> I often think of you and have concluded to write you a short note—if it only should tell how I love, and what a treat it would be to see you all. . . . Be gentle with one another—do all you can to make others happy and you will thereby make yourselves the happier. Love Mama—take good care of her—let her have a good time.
> Your affectionate Father

*Harry Phipps in Ceylon, 1879*

Harry Phipps loved to travel. His first trip abroad had been in 1866, when at age twenty-seven, after considerable introspection and twelve years of uninterrupted work, he allowed himself the luxury of a vacation tour of Europe. It was the trip of a lifetime. Andrew Carnegie, J. W. Vandevort (another close Carnegie friend), and Harry "visited most of the capitals of Europe," wrote Carnegie in his autobiography, "and in all enthusiasm of youth climbed every spire, slept on mountain-tops, and carried our luggage in knapsacks upon our backs. We ended our journey upon Vesuvius where we resolved some day to go around the world."

This trip was but the first of many Atlantic crossings that Harry and Andrew would make, sometimes together and often apart. In 1881, when Carnegie returned in triumph to his Scottish birthplace, there atop the coach as it sailed into Dunfermline was Harry Phipps, sitting with the brothers Tom and Andrew, and their mother Margaret Carnegie. Harry was there to share the fulfillment of Andrew's childhood dream, back in Allegheny, when riding in a carriage had "seemed to us to embrace everything known as wealth and most of what was worth striving for. Father and mother [Carnegie] would not only be seen in Pittsburgh, but should visit Dunfermline, their old home, in style."[1] And so they did.

During the 1867 trip, the three aspiring young capitalists, away from the confinement of Allegheny's "little hells of steel," had been exposed for the first time to a vast cultural world. Rather than recoiling from culture shock, they had been quick to recognize that refinement of their taste through the enlightenment of travel would be beneficial.

That first trip had given Phipps, shy and retiring by nature, a thirst for a greater knowledge of the distant world, its geography, literature, and arts. In travel, he sought to augment his limited childhood education. Countries he had only read about could now be experienced first hand. While other industrial giants of his generation would use their new-found wealth to entertain lavishly, to pursue sport, or to collect great art, Harry's only respite from work was travel. Even so, his trips were always "partly for

1. Carnegie, *Autobiography*, p. 56.

*First tour of Europe, 1866:* from left, *Harry Phipps, Andrew Carnegie, and J. W. Vandevort*

business and partly for pleasure." He would arrive in a new city early in the morning, and quickly complete his scheduled business—looking after the Carnegie Steel investments—while the rest of the day was spent exploring and sightseeing at a leisurely pace. At night, in the quiet of his hotel room, he would sift through and analyze what he had seen and share it all in a letter to Annie and his children.

He acquired an experienced eye in evaluating the places he saw, especially in America. In 1889, during a California trip, he visited San Diego and wrote Annie that the city "perhaps not in my day, will be one of the great cities of America—the [Panama] Canal will be built & then SD will spring into greatness." Nor was it just cities that captured his interest. "If I was a farmer," he wrote in the same

*Andrew Carnegie making his triumphal return to Dunfermline, Scotland, 1881: on the driver's seat are,* from left, *Andrew*

*Carnegie, his mother Margaret, and partner Harry Phipps; Tom Carnegie is seen just behind his brother.*

*The Baptistry, Pisa, Italy, 1893*

*Harry and Jay in Göteberg, Sweden, c. 1882*

*In Austria:* on third step, *Amy;* on fifth step, right, *Helen;* left of Helen, *Annie*

*A family group in the Colosseum, Rome, 1893*

*Myrtle House, Digby, Nova Scotia, 1889*

*Harry,* right, *visiting Mount Vernon, 1899*

*Harry,* left, *and Annie,* on carriage step, *in Moscow, c. 1890*

*Franz Josef Fountain, Graz, Austria, 1893*

letter, "California would be my home so far as my judgment can see. Greater gains & less labor and more comfort than attend the husbandman in colder climate."

The people too impressed him. While in Winnemucca, Nevada, in 1888, he found that "the pluck, energy and enterprise of the people are very remarkable." However, he could not help but note that "the refinement and the morals of the people are not equal to the longer settled States. This is what may be expected from a new Country, but not such a place as would attract me in which to bring up a family—too mu⬤ rudeness—drinking and disregard of Sunday."

Because his business often took him outside the United States, it was not long before he had kept that 1867 promise, made on the slopes of Vesuvius, to go around the world. Travel by sea, rail, and road was slow, but between 1888 and 1895, a steady stream of Harry's letters flowed home from Berlin, Bologna, Bombay, Cairo, Calcutta, Carthage, Ceylon, Gibraltar, Jerusalem, Lisbon, Liverpool, London, Madrid, Marseilles, Naples, Paris, Rome, Singapore, Tangiers, and Yokohama.

He apparently thrived on the hectic pace he set. According to one busy 1895 itinerary, "My journey from Chicago begins at 10:30 pm today and ends at Salt Lake City at 1 am Tuesday morning. A day & night there, then 60 hours to San Francisco and 24 more to Pasadena. . . . *I am feeling first rate!*" Over and over, his letters told the family how much he enjoyed his trips. The same man who at other times wrote so critically of business matters and so admonishingly to his children, always found "the air . . . an appetizer—and stimulating like champagne" when traveling. Even when he fell victim to a common adversity of travel, as he did in Chicago in 1893, he could write to Jay with jocularity rather than annoyance:

Who do you think had a pocket picked? Your father in the train en route to the City. Getting off at Van Buren St., I was crowded and asked

a man to let me pass and he answered "Oh, you want to get off—excuse me" and I felt a sort of squeeze. . . . I felt for my pocketbook. It was gone & so was the train. Lost $35 to $45. Gain—Experience! Will put the bulk of my money inside my vest pocket, my old practice.

Harry might not have indulged his passion for travel had it not been for the callings of his business,

*Harry and Annie Phipps in Egypt, 1890*

*Harry and Annie in the Court of Lions, the Alhambra, Granada, Spain, 1894*

*The Alhambra, 1894*

for above all else, he was a devoted husband and family man. While the children were young, he and Annie both agreed that her place was with them, although Harry often sorely missed her companionship. Each anniversary spent apart, he would write or cable, one year calling their wedding day "the day on which took place the happiest event of my life." And one New Year's Eve found him alone in a hotel room, wishing he were home. The next best thing was penning a letter to his Annie, confiding to her that although "the flora of this region . . . is now remarkable for its beauty and variety—have often plucked the flowers—but where's the use when you have not a lovely lady with you to enjoy them?"

By 1884, Annie was at last free enough from the responsibilities of motherhood to travel with Harry. Over the years, she accompanied him on approximately one third of the trips he made. She quickly adapted to the whirlwind touring style of her husband, and together they explored the wonders of the world, always trying to experience the lifestyle for themselves, now dressing in native garb, now

sleeping in tents along the Nile. Harry, Annie, and the children who sometimes accompanied them were typical nineteenth-century American tourists. They traveled with little concern for their social position or wealth, delighting in the everyday pleasure of ordinary tourist attractions.

"We came here yesterday," Annie wrote to Jay from Cairo in 1890, "Amy and I driving [a cart] and Papa on a donkey. The donkeys are very easy to ride here; their gait is said to be like that of the camels. Today we climbed to the top of Cheops and visited the Temple of the Sphinx."

During a trip to the Alhambra in Granada, Harry and Annie, like so many tourists before and after them, read Washington Irving's *Tales of the Alhambra.* It fired their imaginations and prompted Harry to describe the Alhambra, that Moorish paradise, to Jay as "a dream of beauty, and this Country is or has been a land of romance, song and chivalry, and they still seem to linger with it, especially if the imagination is aided, as ours has been with a copy of Washington Irving's *Alhambra.* Your mother is sitting near me & is enjoying the book I mention."

Annie had little trouble accepting this new part

*Harry and Annie in moorish dress, the Alhambra, 1894*

*North Mymms Park, England, c. 1890:* seated, from left, *Annie and Helen Phipps; an unidentified cousin; Margaret and John Shaffer; another cousin; Frank Hoffstot;* standing, from left, *Amy and Howard Phipps; Annie's sister Addie Shaffer Hoffstot (with baby); Harry, and Hal Phipps*

*Tennis at North Mymms Park, c. 1890: Harry,* second from left, *Howard,* center, *Amy,* seated, right center, *and Annie,* standing

*North Mymms Park, c. 1890:* standing, from right, *Amy; two friends; Harry Phipps; Annie Phipps is seated beside Harry, her daughter Helen to her left and son Howard, third from right*

of her life despite its rigor. In 1891, on a coaching trip through England, she found that such travel "makes one very sleepy as well as very hungry!" as she wrote to Jay. "Tomorrow we cross the Bristol Channel in a train—the ferry is not in use now. It will give my horses a light day. In our coaching trip everything is perfect, there is nothing we can ask further for our pleasure. Every day seems to add to our enjoyment." Wherever they were, she was happy, particularly if other members of the family were also along. "Amy, Helen & Howard had a fine time in Burma," she wrote from aboard the *Arcadia* as it steamed out of Bombay. "The ship is monotonous but restful."

Eventually such travels included the entire family, especially after 1891 when Harry and Annie sold their Allegheny home. Because their five children had been born there and their earliest times together had been spent there, it was not without a certain sadness that they parted from the place.

"Selling our home," wrote Harry to Jay, "though expected and long desired yet causes a pang; a home which I enjoyed and from which I expected to be carried to my last one, is now the property of another, the severing of such ties and the separation of a lifetime association with Allegheny cannot but create a feeling of regret." Harry and Annie were not to own another home until 1903.

Without a real home base, travel became a way of life for the whole family as they traversed the continents, from boarding schools to fashionable resorts, from Britain's great estates to the capitals of the world. Often Harry would be crossing the Atlantic one way while Annie and the children were on a ship heading the other way. During these years, the pattern of letter writing that Harry had established on his solitary trips

*Outside Knebworth House, c. 1892: Harry and Annie are standing, behind the carriage*

*Helen,* left, *at Knebworth, c. 1892*

*Hal,* left, *and Howard with their dogs, outside Knebworth House, c. 1892*

*Hal, c. 1892, standing before Knebworth House, family home of Sir Edward Bulwer-Lytton*

*North Mymms Park, c. 1890:* seated from left, *Amy, John Shaffer, Addie Hoffstot with her three children, Margaret Shaffer, and Howard;* standing from left, *Helen, Frank Hoffstot, Hal, Annie, and Harry*

*The fishing cottage at Knebworth, c. 1892*

became the focus of the family. Now, the network of letters bound the family together and formed the nucleus of family communication, substituting for what in the average home was daily discussion around the dinner table.

Through these letters, each member of the family kept abreast of family news. They communicated all the events of their daily lives, the health of relatives, news of old friends and of those newly made, and lists of travel itineraries and schedules. Typical is a letter from Annie to Harry in 1893, in which she begins by telling him that "the boys have been to the circus in Liverpool. . . . The weather is rather foggy but much better than London. Both Hal and Howard are looking better than when they came from school. . . . I will get Hal tomorrow two good stout pairs of boots with cork soles. I wish almost that I did not have to go to Rome . . . but it would be a disappointment to Amy. I still think that Howard should not go back to school next term but should live as much in the open air as possible."

What had started out as a few lines stretched to eight pages, followed by an even longer letter the next day. Such letters were forwarded from one member of the family to another, round-robin fashion, so that each would be aware of what the others were doing just as if they were indeed gathered around the dining table.

However, Harry and Annie were not always content with the nomadic life of the family. At times it worried them both, as Harry confided to Jay in 1894.

> This life we have been leading for several years, peripatetic, without a country & a home, no tendrils growing & becoming deep and strong, is surely not the best. What do you think? If Mother and I were alone in the World we could choose that land and sky that pleased us best but as it is there are five good reasons why we should seek a permanent home.

Yet, another nine years were to pass before such a place was found, and by then most of the five would have spread their wings and flown.

Annie too questioned the wisdom of so much travel for the children. In writing to her brother, Harvey Shaffer, she told him that "five children of the ages and dispositions of ours require much care & attention from me. I cannot bear to be away from

*Amy,* second from left, *and friends feeding Tommy, the pet fawn, at Knebworth, c. 1893*

*Harry and Annie by the entrance to Knebworth House, c. 1892*

*Helen and Amy,* far right, *with friends, Knebworth, c. 1893*

them a day—and now, they should begin studying in earnest. . . . Travelling about is not the best thing for such young children."

The children themselves may have felt some uneasiness over the family's nomadic ways. "I don't know what I call home," wrote Hal from school in 1894, "but I suppose it is where you all are."

While family unity was sustained by voluminous correspondence, the happiest times were had when the family was together under one roof, albeit a rented one. For several months of the year, they leased one or another of the finest estates in England and Scotland—Knebworth Castle, North Mymms Park, or Beaufort Castle. There, the children were given their first taste of a scale of architecture and a way of life that was the antithesis of their parents' and their own early Allegheny upbringing. They acquired an appreciation for large country houses with formal gardens surrounded by vast acres of open country-side. Each of the children would one day duplicate in their own homes their dreams and memories of the Scottish and English estates.

Nor were Annie and Harry unmoved by these grand surroundings. From Beaufort Castle in 1898, Annie wrote:

> We have a large drawing room 35' wide by 70' long. You can imagine how the music sounds. We expect the pipes here tonight and the young folk will have some dancing. I never saw a more complete house. . . . Harry and I had a ride together this morning. Afterwards we went deer stalking, and got three fine stags. Jay shot two of them. . . . This afternoon eight of us went to a tea party and met a number of delightful people.

Short in duration, lasting usually only the span of a school vacation, these family reunions were moments of great joy for Harry, Annie, and their children. Amy, Jay, Helen, Hal, and Howard filled their days with riding, shooting, fishing, and tennis, each child acquiring a lifelong love for "sport" that would be passed along to their own children. Their passion prompted Harry to write in 1894 that Hal, who spent

*Helen and Amy,* far left, *Annie and Harry,* third and fourth from right, *with Andrew Carnegie,* in hat, *and friends, c. 1888*

44

*Harry on Browny, North Mymms Park, c. 1891*

much time outdoors riding and hunting, "is not as careful as he should be about taking colds. He should be as careful of his health as he is with his horse. If he had a fine horse that was not taken care of, Hal would be *indignant.* Strange how some prize those things of lower value."

Though not an enthusiastic participant in the sports his children enjoyed so much, Harry would on occasion take a quiet ride on his favorite horse, Browny. In 1891, after one particularly "beautiful, lone ride . . . sun, air and clouds lovely," Harry promised Annie that "another year I am going to have a duplicate of Browny for you. I want to have all I need and it is too bad that I have not had you ride with me on a quiet safe horse for these past years." The solitude and tranquility of Mymms Park that day caused Harry to reflect upon what was most important in his fifty-odd years of life. In wanting to "have all I need," he was not being self-indulgent. This was instead a tender expression of his continuing love for Annie and need of her companionship.

In the fall of that same year, as the time ap-

proached for the family to leave Mymms and disperse, Harry wrote to Jay that "the above date [September 9, 1891] tells me how quickly the days go by and what a short time remains for beautiful North Mymms, which will always be like a lovely dream of the past."

In rising above those "little hells of steel" of Allegheny days, as Harry's brother John had prophesied thirty years earlier, the family had certainly found a gracious way of life previously unknown to them. However, as long as Harry held the reins as patriarch of the family, he allowed no ostentatious display of wealth for reasons of social presentment, so common with other newly landed American aristocrats of the period. Future generations of Phippses might search the playgrounds of Europe for the pleasures of society, fashion, and sport, but not Harry. The family's gatherings were strictly private affairs, with relatives and old friends visiting to partake in the "wonderment of nature" by enjoying such simple pleasures as an old-fashioned picnic on the heath. Finding time to relax from the turmoil of business, Harry treasured these months with his family.

*Harry Phipps, c. 1891*

As Harry traveled the world alone, his children were often in his thoughts, but as they were too young yet to understand all that he wished to say to them, he would simply insert a line or two in his letters to Annie. From California for example, after describing the events of the day and plans for the next, he added, "tomorrow we drive to see an Indian settlement & may get a bow & arrows for ? And for whom shall I get a Mexican Saddle, what boy is best? Who deserves it?"

When he did write to one of the children directly, he confined his remarks to news of his travels or to future plans as in this excerpt from a letter to ten-year-old Hal:

> The subject of next Summer's vacation and how to spend it has been for some time in my thoughts—and now I want to consult you. What do you think of this plan—visit the Yellowstone Park and have our own wagons, tents and so forth? . . . We can camp out and make drives of several hundred miles. We can fish and buy game. At night we can put up our tents and sleep very comfortably. A great many people do this . . . Have not decided anything yet—only thinking—suppose you do a little.

*Jay Phipps, c. 1890*

As the children grew, Harry felt that they needed his direct guidance, even though the demands of his business kept them apart most of the time. He began to write more often, and his letters became "arrows of morality." Admonishing, praising, moralizing, he poured out all the anxieties of an absent father. "How a father's heart is drawn to his child," he wrote, "and how he often fears danger when none exist, but better be some time unduly alarmed than oblivious to the surrounding perils, which even the most thoughtless youth will admit."

His children had not experienced poverty as he had, and he feared that they would be spoiled by the family's wealth unless carefully guided. He wrote to Jay in 1894:

> It has often been a wonder to me why the poor boy seeks advice, and the rich man's son neglects or despises it. Cannot fancy any reply justifying it. If the child of fortune thinks help unneeded he is a fool, twice the need is his! Many more pitfalls, the snares, temptations beset him than the poor lad. The luxury of the rich man, his easy hours, his ignorance of business, of the value of money and the tricks of the unscrupulous all lead him to ruin physically, morally and financially. . . . No irony of fate could be worse than for a father to be successful & that prove a curse to his children. Continual effort on their part & continual advice from the parents, are the duties of both.
>
> I am ever your loving & anxious father and looking forward to the time when my Sons—grown in Character, Knowledge & Stature—will make me a proud parent, otherwise may I never see the day that will bring me sorrow & disappointment. Ill health I may survive, the other, *never.*

Each time Harry had to leave his family to travel on business, he left his children with an anxious "farewell" letter, reiterating his reasons for them to adhere to the wisdom of his counsel. In one such

*Jay,* far right, *astride his bicycle, Phillips Academy, Andover, Massachusetts, c. 1888*

letter to Jay, he ended: "I am sorry to leave the country and especially you, but your dear mother is lonely and I am also without her companionship, but it will be one of the most painful things to leave you my dear, dear son. Do your duty, go to bed in good season, rise early, do your duty thoroughly, and remember your father's heart will be broken if you do not lead a noble life."

Jay was to bear the brunt of his father's incessant barrage of Victorian morality. From 1888, when he left home to attend Phillips Academy, Andover, Massachusetts, until 1896 when he graduated from Yale University, he received several such letters each week. The first son out in the world, he was also the primogeniture of the family's fortune, as his father often reminded him: "You are the eldest of whom I expect most. To the end, prove valiant and strong in all your efforts for good. If you had your fortune all in one vessel, would you not be anxious? My greatest fortune is the character & standing of my children. That gone I would care for nothing else."

With what trepidation must young Jay have opened his father's letters. Though interspersed with news and praise, they were intended to weigh upon Jay's conscience and guide his conduct as if his father were present, looking over his shoulder, as he read: "It would be interesting to me if I could, unseen by you, witness your reading this letter. Whether my efforts for your good are appreciated or disliked I

cannot tell, poor helpless earnest anxious loving father, who is striving unselfishly for the good of his son."

Not only was Jay expected to be guided by his father's unseen presence, he was also commanded to respond to each letter by return mail. "Let me have two letters a week," wrote Harry. "One Sunday & one Thursday. . . . When you are replying to a letter, read it over again and answer it item by item, that is business method and the right one, please remember."

If Jay lagged in his responses, his father would fire off a stern letter, addressed to "John" rather than "Jay." Typical is this letter of July 8, 1889:

> Dear John—
>     I am quite disappointed, no letter from you today now for many days—wired you & beg to ask if this is a proper recognition that fond parents expect from a dutiful son—
>     No report from you about your studies—your hours of rising—and retiring—your promptness, progress & etc. Many interesting matters about which you are suspiciously silent—Please wire & explain (as they say in legislative bodies) and free the commanding officer of further trouble.
>     When I was forty years of age I kept my father better advised of my movements. Thoughtlessness is some times inexcusable—write fully—frequently—frankly—and free us from fear as

to how you are doing.

I thought when you had a vacation you would be glad to write us often—

Yrs affy,
HP Jr.

With his eye for detail, Harry reflected upon even the most trivial matters; for example, concerning health, he commented in one letter, "Kind of your cousin to send you candy—but wiser not to send you what will injure your health, temper & teeth," and in another, "Uncle Harvey says your underwear is entirely unsuitable for Winter wear. Please see to this & get the matter righted & have no regrets when too late to repair an injury already done to health."

When Jay had first left home for Andover, Annie too could not help but insert a word of motherly advice into her otherwise newsy letters. She would warn him to "be very careful about what you read" and to "remember that your duty is to learn all the good you can and prepare yourself for the business of life." Nor could she resist reminding him now and then of his father's early struggles, writing that "Papa started to work between fourteen and fifteen years of age, but tried to make up the deficiencies of his

education by going to night school. You have a new school, and all arrangements have been made for your comfort while you work." She also tried to pass along the religious fervor from which she drew strength, telling Jay to "say in your own words each morning, just as you rise, 'Every word that I speakth Every step that I taketh / Wilt Thou guard / I ask / for Christ's Sake'" and adding, "You have not told me whether you go to the Episcopal or Presbyterian Church—I am anxious to know."

Annie's advice was always expressed in a softer voice than Harry's, for she never doubted the moral character of her children or their ability to direct their own lives according to their upbringing. After Jay went on to Yale, Annie's letters to him would contain only cursory advice. For example, during his freshman year, she wrote, "Dear, I must ask you not to drink *beer*. Get all the milk you like but do not get into the habit of taking beer—Trust me, it will do you much more harm than good. Wait until you are much older, you are too young to need that kind of thing."

In contrast, Harry saw Jay's entrance to Yale as a time to step up his efforts to oversee his son's behavior. Yale had a less structured atmosphere than Andover, and Harry feared that Jay might fall under the influence of new friends of whom he would not

From left, *Jay, Howard, and Hal Phipps, c. 1893*

*Amy and Helen, c. 1887*

approve. He wrote to Jay in 1894: "I want you to make a reputation at College, by studying hard, by economy in your expenditures, and not to think of pleasures, but of profit. Avoid all company that is not improving. You are not at that great seat of learning for play, but for business, bear these truths in mind."

The choice of friends was a perennial concern

to Harry. Even before Jay's earlier departure for Andover, Harry had written to him about the possibility of summer guests in England: "If you and Hal find nice friends we *may* later on & near the time invite them one for each of you to make us a visit if we take an English Country home next summer." Much later, but before Jay graduated from Yale, Harry continued to exert his influence in this area. In one letter, which reached Jay just as he was about to embark for England to join the family, Harry wrote, "You are now on the threshold of manhood and ought to know . . . what is proper and becoming but a number of young men travelling together sometimes forget themselves and act like apes. Unless they are all gentlemen . . . I beg to ask you to change your ship & come in preference with strangers." Apparently, Harry's concern even encompassed the choice of pets for, in the same letter, he continued: "I wrote you not to bring your dog! I should be ashamed to see a son of mine with a bull-dog. I look upon it as showing a low coarse taste. A man's companions show what he is. I told your Mother, Genl Grant's son-in-law would prove a bad one—loved fisticuffs and had a bulldog, the results were what I feared, never found it otherwise. Fifty-odd years should be wiser than twenty."

With Jay at Yale, Harry advised him to be careful not to go to "every race or gathering of that kind . . . as they are attended by swearers, smokers, drinkers, gamblers, etc. not the crowd that a good earnest man should seek. There are enough pitfalls that open unexpectedly under our feet, without going to the place where they most abound." He warned Jay to "dismiss from your companionship unsuitable men and from your thoughts every thing that will not strengthen you in life's battle." He suggested that "if you should find your environment is bad, if possible, change it, or come straight away home where you will ever find a warm welcome. Education is all very well but character is indispensable, without which, life is nothing." Harry was unwilling to entrust matters of his children's moral conduct to any other authority than himself. Not even the renowned Yale University would do:

*Hal at Knebworth, c. 1894*

> September 4, 1893
> My Dear Son,
>     In sending you to College I am giving you every opportunity—and I wish you to miss none. The chances of advancement you possess were unfortunately denied to me, much to my serious disadvantage through life. It will be the sorrow of my life, if you do not make a fine record, maintain your health and increase your strength. I write soberly and seriously . . . However, the matter of your education is trifling as compared to heeding my directions. Please remember this & may you ever be guided and guarded from all evil, that too often destroy College youths . . . morally, mentally and physically. Ever your loving father,
> HP Jr.

*Helen, c. 1894*

Throughout Jay's school years, Harry used love, conscience, and command to prod his son to behave according to his wishes. The details of the day-to-day routine took on importance under a father's stern eye:

February 3, 1984

My Dear Son,

No letter, but I presume you are busy and am always willing to wait, when that is the case.

Hope you spend your evenings at home & go early to bed. I am really anxious on these points. Of course in these important matters as long as you are a minor & drawing supplies from me, I will expect more faithfulness to my wishes than from an employee whose future is dependent on me. . . . Am well. Much love dear boy,

Yrs always,
HP Jr.

At other times, Harry warned Jay of the dire consequences of ignoring a father's advice. Such predictions could be terrifying in their life-and-death intensity:

My Dear Son,

This is my Birthday, another mile stone reached in the long and important journey of life. Everything has gone well with me, and my only anxiety, and an absorbing one it is, [is] for the welfare of my boys, that no seas of trouble or temptation may overwhelm them. . . .

Be you wise as the coachman who said he drove far from the danger line, so you keep far from temptation, and it will never reach you; the reverse policy means ruin to yourself, and illness if not perhaps death to one of your parents if not both. Mother and I can meet with bravery all troubles, but those of sufferings which come from the ill doing of our boys, for such sorrows, there is no balm no comfort, but that which comes from the last sleep. Plain talking now may spare much agony hereafter. The stab would strike us first, and then perhaps yourself with increased bitterness, and your lot I would not have for the World

Ever so much love, my dear Jay—
HP Jr.

As much as Jay loved his father, he could never meet the exacting standard of perfection demanded. No one could. There was no questioning the wisdom of his father's advice once separated from the Victorian overtones of impending doom should he fail to live up to it. It was simply more than any boy in Jay's situation could comfortably live with if he had any

*Annie in 1895*

conscience at all. Over and over again, for eight years, he read the same demands: "one hundred percent effort and performance seven days a week . . . be first in your class . . . set the perfect example for your brothers . . . keep far from temptation . . . go early to bed . . . miss no opportunity to advance . . . stand straight . . . maintain your health, increase your strength . . . no billious suppers, bad companions or late hours . . . do your duty thoroughly, lead a noble life."

How could Jay ever answer his father and appease such anxiety? He chose to take Harry's probings literally and answer with an hour-by-hour account of his weekly activities in a letter to his mother:

> September 16, 1891
>
> Dearest Mother,
>
> I received two of Father's letters today and one yesterday. I am going to write one short letter every day so that you will know exactly how we are getting along, and I hope never have to worry again. We rise at 7 and breakfast at 7.30. At 8.45 school begins. We commence with English with Dr. L. which lasts one hour, then we have Geometry with him which lasts another hour. At 10.45 to 11—we have a recess. At 11 we take Latin and French on alternate days; and from 12 to 1 German every day. We have dinner at 1.15—over at 2. From 2 to 4 we take walks. From 4 to 6.30 we study and from 6.30 to 7 practice on the violin. At 7 we have Supper and at 8 we study till 9.30. Lights out at 10 P.M. Saturday free.
>
> Sunday English day. This is the plan we have until Christmas. . . . With loads of love to all.
>
> Your affectionate son,
> Jay

Annie happily read her son's letter, underlining and correcting any misspelled words as was her habit with all her children's letters. Before she mailed it back to Jay, she shared it with Harry, who, far more interested in content than spelling, immediately replied: "You say you have Saturday free! Do you mean to say that then the day will be lost and nothing to show for it? If you do, you do not appreciate your position and your duties to yourself and your parents."

Although Jay had purposely chosen a superficial response to his father's inquiries so as to avoid any conflict, he had left a loophole through which his father could bring the matter back into its proper perspective. There was no circumventing Harry's wish for perfection of his son's character.

With the other children, Harry was not as demanding but he did expect them to follow his advice. Hal, age fifteen and away at school, answered his father's anxious letters quite differently:

> April 7, 1894
>
> My dearest Father,
>
> I received your letter that you so kindly sent me with so much good advice to-day & will try & follow it to the Letter. I cannot make my letters so long as yours because there is nothing much going on here just now; I don't mean that I am not doing any work but that there is no general news of importance enough to write to you about. As to reading your dear letters, why I always read & reread them & love to receive them for their own worth & because they make some of the boys envious—I think. I am sorry you think my letters are mere scribblings. . . . I am quite well & hope you can say the same of the rest. I'm afraid I have neglected dear little Mother, because I have not written to her for some time. Please give her my dearest love. . . . I am beginning to think letter (at least home letter writing) writing is a pleasure instead as I have always thought a hardship. It makes you think more of home. . . . It is getting near preparation time & shall have to stop although I do not want to when once I get fairly started.
>
> With dearest love to yourself and all the rest, I remain,
>
> Always your loving son,
> Hal
>
> P.S. Thanks very much for your letter.

Throughout the letter, Hal is careful to qualify everything he says. He explains his short letters by the dearth of news and is forthright in acknowledging his neglect and inadequacy as a correspondent. He uses flattery and affection, and, in calling letter writing a pleasure and professing to learn from his father's letters, Hal had told his father just what he wanted to hear. Harry welcomed and accepted Hal's explanations even though the wool had been pulled over his eyes momentarily. Harry's enthusiasm over Hal's response to his advice found its way into a letter to Jay: "Can you believe it? Hal actually enjoys my letters and is getting to like writing back." However, Jay's letters were far more carefully scrutinized than were Hal's, for it was Jay, the eldest son, upon whom Harry had placed his hopes for the future of the family. An indulgent response to Hal was therefore of no great consequence.

Harry's daughters, Amy and Helen, were under the close guidance of Annie or relatives, and they caused him little concern. He undoubtedly felt that their upbringing was better left in a mother's hands to meet their role in life and gave his views on the subject in a letter to Jay, explaining that

> the girls also have lessons in music and Italian. Amy is having her portrait painted in pastel. Helen looks very well, has a pleasant manner.

From left, *Amy; a Shaffer cousin; and Jay at North Mymms Park, c. 1891*

Amy talks of going to a Childs Hospital; Dr. Browne of London is eager to aid me in arranging the matter. A woman should be as thoroughly equipped as a man for future duties, and few or none are as important, as Knowledge of nursing. A sine qua non in my opinion, if Woman is to be a "ministering angel", and *all should aim to be.*

However, Harry expected his daughters to write to him, if only to send news of their daily lives. As early as age nine, Amy was writing:

My Dear Papa,

Howard is getting washed and is as good as a kitting. I have written two letters to Mamma, and am going to write to you. It is a lovely morning and Charlie is singing with all his might.

Don't you think I could ride horseback? Thank you for the books. In the first one were two lovely continued stories. Please send me the next number.

Ninety dollars gone to smash. The pony is dead. We have a swing in the barn.

I am going to town to see Mamma today. We are all really well. All send love to Pappa and cousin Jennie and many kisses.

With love,
Amy

It's very hard to keep from eating green apples!

*Howard at Knebworth, c. 1894*

At age eleven, Helen wrote a similarly newsy letter from the Grand Hotel, Point Chautauqua, where "its lovely . . . now. Its so cool and there are lots of girls too. I go in bathing every day with another girl named Emma. We have lots of fun with the boats. We get in them while they are tied and rock it with all our mite. Mama went out with Jay at half past six to fish. Jay caught three and Mama caught one. I am going out now so good-by. My love 0 0 0 0 0 kisses—Helen."

Should Harry not hear from his daughters, especially when they were away at school, he would anxiously send off a mild letter of reproach, without the condemning overtones of his letters to his sons. Amy, at age fourteen, answered such a note by adding a postscript to a letter to her mother, "Tell dear Papa I am very sorry I made him so nervous by keeping him waiting."

As the two girls grew older, they began to find their father's letters less menacing, almost quaint. Amy wrote of this in a letter to her father just after Christmas, 1893:

> My dearest Father,
>
> Many many thanks for the Charming little book I received this morning. We have had a very happy Christmas here [Rome], though naturally we missed you all very much. . . . It was a happy day but it didn't really seem like Christmas with us all scattered at the four corners of the earth. I do hope next year we shall all be together. . . . Helen and I also received your dear funny characteristic business letter! It is so like you and so kind. Helen and I had to laugh, it is exactly the way you talk—if I had heard it without knowing who had written it I am sure I should have recognized it! . . . With much love from us both—
>> Your loving,
>> Amy

Howard, the youngest and last child at home, was spared his father's letters of morality. He was only three when Harry began to write them in 1884 and still at home when the letters ended in 1895. However, during these years, there was always some news of "dear little Howard," his poor teeth or broken bones, in Harry's letters to the other children. Interspersed with advice and guidance, words of praise about Howard's progress were as predictable as mention of the weather. Harry was spending more time with the family in these later years, and he enjoyed the personal contact with his youngest son. To watch a child grow up was a new experience, one that he had completely missed with his other children.

At age fifty-eight, Harry showed signs of mellowing and tiring, and his letters became briefer than they had been. Five children had already been "launched on the important journey of life," and he had poured out his heart in more than a thousand letters to them over a ten-year period, with the fervent hope that "plain talking now may spare much agony hereafter in life's long oftime laborious path."

*Howard, c. 1885, and the record of an early business venture*

As a parting affirmation of his belief in the moral advice contained in his letters, he penned a short note to Jay, just before his son's graduation from Yale in 1896:

> I want my son to be a noble man, to do nothing that would please an enemy, or some butterfly companion, the friend of an hour and not of a lifetime as a parent is. Please save my letters, if you don't often read them, return them to me and I will seal them up for others when I am gone.

Jay did keep his father's letters, however much they may have plagued him as a youngster; they rested quietly in a trunk in Westbury House attic for three quarters of a century waiting to be read by another generation.

*Jay Phipps at Yale University, c. 1894*

# HP JR. ECONOMICS

Content to leave Jay's liberal arts education to Andover and Yale, Harry Phipps personally oversaw his son's instruction in the value of money and its management. After all, a keen understanding of finance had been his making, and he set about to instill in young Jay the proper respect for the fortune he would one day inherit, with the "fond hope that the time will soon come when you will be as careful with thousands of dollars on hand as tho you had but little."

This new undertaking went hand in hand with Harry's other efforts at shaping his children's character. He believed that "the man who takes care of himself, morally, mentally, physically and financially is the one most fitted to survive!" Having stressed moral, mental, and physical development for several years in letters to the children, he now turned to remedy their financial inexperience. He often reminded them of their position, writing, for example, "Remember you have never earned y'r money & it is plain you cannot fully appreciate its value. Laboring and struggling for money makes its value known, and an experience of needing and not having money is worth much to a young man or woman."

Thus, in 1893, the treasurer and financial genius of Carnegie Steel singled out his eldest son, then at Yale, and, using advice and artful manipulation of the purse strings, gave him a three-year course in economics. He wrote to Jay that "now is the time to learn the use and value of money. Any sane man can learn it. The faculty I mention will outweigh anything that Yale can give." This was a long, unbending course—often unpleasant for Jay—but always with the promise that upon graduation, he would reap the rewards of his deprivation and self-denial. As Harry stated his purpose:

> It is my wish to give you every right comfort & enjoyment that is compatible with your progress & making a man of you, this is all I aim at. My money I could not take with me, but its use must not be in a manner to injure you by habits of extravagance. Any economies you make, I will pay you on your 21st birthday to make you a good permanent investment— Remember this—! So you are not saving for me, but for yrself.

*Harry Phipps, c. 1894*

The cornerstone of the course was the monthly ledger that Jay was to keep. In it he listed all monies received from his father and "all disbursements and what part is charged to me [Harry] and what to your allowance so we may get a starting point." Their agreement was that Jay receive a monthly allowance of $150 to cover certain personal expenses and that he charge other specified costs to the Phipps office for Harry's review and payment. The arrangement is outlined in Harry's letter of December 7, 1893: "I think as *you* suggested that I pay certain bills. Say Tuition, board, lodging, home at Xmas and going home at Easter, the other allowance you receive and disburse. The 'Allowance' I should be glad to know how you use it—but if you prefer not to make it known, which I think is important in teaching you careful method and business way, I will waive my request until further notice."

*Jay,* front row, *with his infamous bulldog at Yale University*

*Jay's room at Yale, the walls festooned with pictures from home*

*Jay,* middle row, third from left, *with his Yale classmates, c. 1893*

Left on his own to learn financial responsibility, as his father wished, Jay actually had an unlimited credit line, for all bills could be directed to the Phipps office for payment. Spending was constrained only by the keeping of the ledger and his father's earlier advice: "If you have any—pay all debts—let no bills follow you. 'Pay as you go' is the best advice anyone can give to young or old. Getting into debt is like running downhill, easy to do but hard to get up again. With credit much much more is bought than needed."

Perhaps not surprisingly, after the first year, Jay ran into trouble keeping his ledger balanced and was admonished by his father:

> I was preparing to write you when my cash receipts & disbursements acc't was received for November which put me to seriously thinking.
>
> Formerly you were very careful about how you spent my money. I admired your spirit in that respect very much, am very sorry to see the change. You are now no longer a boy, but have reached manhood's years & I expect that judgment and carefulness that should mark those years. Until you show how to take care of money & show it by your reports I now notify you to never draw above $200—in any one month.
>
> 2nd. Send me your report bi-weekly
>
> 3rd. If you need more than $200—write me & I will send it to you if deemed best that you should have it.

*Jay, c. 1893*

Jay was not being artful or deceitful in his overspending but just forgetful and perhaps careless in his eagerness to enjoy the same lifestyle and pleasures as his peers at Yale. Harry knew this. He had given the purse strings a gentle tug only because he believed self-denial must be experienced by Jay if the boy was to understand the value of money. With this thought in mind, Harry wrote Jay in 1894 that his "*expensive* account has been gone over, and does not bear evidence of any great self-denial on your part, I am sorry to say. Try and learn the value of money, and do not buy everything you take a fancy to. . . . You should save and do some good with money not all selfishly." He softened his criticism by ending the letter, "If you were not so dear to me, I would not trouble you with so much advice. Heed it and you will never regret it."

Often a particular item in Jay's ledger would be singled out as an example of what Harry considered needless extravagance, such as a pair of expensive gloves from a fashionable New Haven clothier charged to the office. Confronted with the bill, Harry wrote to his son, demanding, "Shall I pay this bill? Am surprised if you would pay $5.50 for gloves!

Terribly expensive! As soon lost and as easy blackened. . . . Never in my life have I ever gone into a strange shop and bought a pair of gloves or small item and had it charged. I would have gone with cold hands for days e'er doing this."

Obviously upset by his father's displeasure, Jay returned the gloves to the store only to be further admonished: "I don't know that it was nice to return them. If the seller objects, enclose him in a registered letter the $5 in a note and 50¢ in stamps. . . . & excuse yourself for trouble given."

It was not the need for new gloves that Harry questioned but a lack of judgment on Jay's part. To compound what might have been dismissed as a mere extravagance had Jay made the purchase with his own very generous allowance, the boy had had the bill sent to the office for payment, thereby indulging in a luxury he could not afford. These were irresponsible actions as far as HP Jr. economics were concerned. To control the situation better, Harry again pulled on the purse strings. He had already gone from monthly to biweekly ledger reports, and now he requested a weekly accounting from Jay, saying, "You are spending annually a sum of money, which you cannot expect for

*At Yale, dressed for tennis, c. 1894*

many years to earn the half of it. Let me make plain to you, it is not the money I begrudge but your foolish lack of management & yet you grumbled about giving me an account of where my money had gone, in some cases wasted. Send me cash accounts *weekly* & each item dated."

Henceforth, Jay's ledger was neatly kept, dutifully submitted, and meticulously scrutinized by his father. One long letter to Jay is typical of the care Harry gave his son's accounts.

My dear son,
. . . Money: I wish I could send you with-

out JW & Rob knowing of y'r great expenditures. As it is, the amounts go on my books under y'r name, where the charges will stand for indefinite years, trumpet tongued to proclaim your wastefulness and extravagance, and if your career is not a success friends will say "what could you expect with such a father's indulgence."

Expense Account: Cab to hotel $1.60, was not that unnecessary, when StCars and ElRd nearby? Tips at Hotel—what may become yr father may be extravagance in you. 2 tickets Yale-Harvard game $5—why such liberality when you earn not a dollar? Magazines and papers, of course, buy some, but best join a library—much cheaper. 3 tickets to Theatre $4.50—ridiculous. You go too much & spend too much on Amusements. . . . 2 Suppers at Heubs $1.90—this nonsense has got to stop, be moderate—wait till you have earned your money.

You certainly do have the sweets & enjoyment of life and ought to be able & willing to work hard in return.

In any item of expense coming up, have you ever said "I cannot afford it," let me know. . . .

Postage. Sometimes under paid & I have to pay *double*. . . .

Teapot & stand, $2.50. What do you need it for? You could have saved $2 on it.

Mousetraps, how many have you now? *4 or more?*

Let me enquire—do you ever deny yourself anything?

Are you a faithful steward making a right use of my money? You should pay back the money that is used wastefully.

What avails Book education, if you have not common sense & know not how to take care of your pocketbook.

Buy no clothes you can possibly avoid, deny y'rself as much as you can & make amends for yr waste. I do not send you to College to have you throw money, helter skelter.

If you say others show you these attentions *don't accept them.* You are having entirely too much play & makes Jack a dull boy! You need not tell me you cannot help these outlays, thousands do & you *must.*

HP Jr.

It is a painful task writing you complaining, urging etc. I hope my reward will be commensurate to my pain and anxiety.

Though at times unfair in his judgment of particular items in the ledger and overbearing in his criticism of his son's spending habits, Harry clearly meant to lay the foundation that would make Jay as adept as he was in managing the vast sums of money that he would soon be turning over to Jay. Once convinced that the lessons had been learned, Harry kept his promise to return to his son all that he had withheld. Beginning in 1895, he increased Jay's allowance to three thousand dollars annually. In thanking his father, Jay also acknowledged, as part of the agreement between father and first-born, "the following conditions: no part of the money at any time to be lent or given by me to any of the other children, & thereby thwart your intention in respect to your allowance to them. I agree to keep full, true, neat & correct account of my expenditures & try to live with reasonable economy & save what I can to the good for investment." On the same page, Harry penned a quick reply: "My dear son, your statement of our understanding is correct."

After Yale, Jay went on to study law at Harvard, and on January 1, 1899, Harry further increased his son's allowance to five thousand dollars, "with the hope it may add to your comfort & enjoyment and increase the show of savings at the end of the century." The following year, Harry began to turn over large sums of money to Jay, beginning with $100,000, followed by a $600,000 gift. Over the next three years, Harry willingly returned to his son, "with pleasure in keeping my promise," bonds and funds representing many times over what Jay had been deprived of during the three-year economics course.

Upon Jay's marriage to Margarita Grace in 1903, Harry wrote simply:

> My dear Son,
>    I have now arranged to give you as a wedding present from Mother and me the sum of Two Million Dollars. . . . indulging the fond hope that you may manage this sum with wisdom and that it will prove a blessing to you and to those most dear to you and in some degree be a boon to lessen the suffering of the unfortunate.
>
> I am yours affectionately,
> Henry Phipps

Jay would never forget the sense of value his father had so painstakingly taught him. Later, he would draw from his early lessons in making purchases, whether they be stocks, land, racehorses, or antiques. However, it was in his routine handling of finance that he was most reminiscent of his father. In running the estate at Old Westbury, Jay arranged for his office to pay all bills and send him a weekly accounting. He would approve or disapprove each item, making notes in the margin, which the office in turn passed along to his estate superintendent. Like his father, Jay often singled out individual items for

*At Yale, dressed for riding, c. 1894*

review. For example, in 1931, the office wrote to Charles Johnson, then the superintendent: "On January 26th, you purchased 200 lbs. New Scrap Hose @ 6¢ per pound from Sam Kantor which you state on the bill was used for wiring trees. Mr. Phipps has underlined the 'new' and would like to know if you can buy *old* hose."

If Jay felt that the men on the estate were growing careless with his property, he would send off a terse note, through the office. One such letter, to Johnson in 1931, said: "Mr. John S. Phipps wishes you to get a loose-leaf notebook and make a complete inventory of every tool you have. When a tool is useless, lost or

*A page from Jay's ledger*

*Jay, c. 1895, with the horse he kept stabled in New Haven*

*Jay,* fourth from left, *and friends from Yale, duck hunting on Long Island Sound in the 1890s*

broken, Mr. Phipps wishes you to make a notation in the inventory. He does not wish you to buy a new tool unless you already have none like it. Please explain this to the carpenters, gardeners, etc."

Borrowing from the same techniques his father had used with him, Jay wanted to assure that his office and estate employees learned a "sense of value" in handling his property with care. What his father had once demanded of him, he now demanded of others. At times, when he wrote to the office it was as though his father guided his hand:

March 8, 1934

Dear Mr. Robbins:

I am returning the receipts enclosed with Charlie Johnson's payrolls of March 8th and 16th. . . . I note some of these bills are not for small amounts and Johnson should get requisitions approved before giving large orders.

I note that one of the bills covers the purchase of one drum of alcohol—$29.30. Tell Johnson that this is a large bill and that he should not order so much alcohol at one time. A drum seems a very large amount for use in the trucks and there must be considerable waste in storage by evaporation. Have any of the employees been using this drum for their own cars?

Yours very truly,
John S. Phipps

In such careful scrutiny of weekly accounts, Jay nurtured and achieved a reputation for being "a hard man . . . tight with the dollar . . . not one to put something over on." During the Depression years, he often laid off men or lowered salaries on his estate payroll without warning in his efforts to contain costs. At the same time, the weekly reports include many notations showing Jay's concern for the welfare of his loyal employees in those hard times. For example, when asked by the office in one 1933 report whether or not to pay an employee who had been out sick for three weeks, Jay responded, "Yes, when a man is sick he needs more than when he is well." While in his handling of small details he may have prided himself on his toughness, he could also act with fairness and a kind heart, in matters of importance.

*Harry Phipps in Ceylon, 1899*

# THE OFFICE

By 1904, Jay, at the age of thirty and assisted by George Gordon of the Phipps office, was running the day-to-day operations of the family's business interests, though still under the watchful eye of his father. Jay was permitted to make any transaction "up to one thousand dollars" on his own, but Harry expected to be consulted on all matters above that amount. Harry's business correspondence with his son, which continued unabated, now contained daily gleanings from the upper echelons of the financial world in which Harry traveled. He fed Jay background information that would help in making sound investment decisions:

> A rumour that Mr. Morgan was ill put down the shares of Steel today a dollar or more. Today I attended my first meeting of the Steel Board. It is marvellous the success of the Company. . . . Mr. Westinghouse spoke to me about wanting to borrow five hundred and fifty thousand dollars ($550,000), and he suggested that he would buy the Traction Securities Company's stock, and pay 5% on it from the time of our payments, which brings me in thirty-three thousand dollars ($33,000), and frees me from what has been so long a dead investment. . . . A few days ago I called to see Mr. Pierpont Morgan and be told I could not sell the Malone Bonds at better than par. At the time demand money was from ten to twenty-five percent, so I concluded not to offer the bonds until perhaps the 1st of January when there will be an investment demand for this kind of security. I asked Mr. Morgan about the Mercantile Marine, and he said it was doing first rate.

*Jay Phipps, c. 1899, Harvard Law School graduate*

Harry's correspondence also encompassed the world of politics with its inevitable repercussions in the business arena. During the Theodore Roosevelt administration, he noted that "the President continues to occasionally make bad breaks in his messages, and is exceedingly unpopular with the business men, and I think he will soon be unpopular with the working classes when they find the consequences that flow from his indiscreet speeches and messages."

Though no longer involved in the daily running of the Phipps office, Harry kept a watchful eye out for signs of waste and extravagance. However minute the infraction, he was quick to quell the matter with one of his familiar admonishing letters to Jay:

> Mr. Bradley Martin Jr. mentioned yesterday that he had to pay such excessive postage charges on letters forwarded by my office. In one case I think fifty to seventy-five cents, and I am enclosing a piece of one envelope where I paid nearly a dollar. I presume the young men have scales, and I wish they would use them, as it is annoying to have these extra charges occur.

Because many of Harry's business letters to his son were confidential, he would often request that Jay "carefully burn all the old statements, as it would be very ugly if they got into the hands of unfriendly people. Be always careful to have them under lock and key." Harry's inbred secretiveness stemmed from his early steel days when a leak of information could result in "costly loss of advantage . . . or disaster." He was uncomfortable with the new business practices of dictation and typewritten letters (with carbon copies so readily available to others), and he considered the telegraph not only expensive but too public for business matters. If expediency necessitated using it, he sent all messages, especially those regarding stock transactions, in his own special code. He would wire, for example, "Standeth freeminded catacomb," which decoded meant, "We have bought 100 consolidated Ga Cot. at $150." Except for Jay, the family apparently did not understand, or at least remember, the code. When Amy received a 1905 telegram reading, "Several chaplaincy extremely befrayment," she sent it to Jay with a note, "Dear Jay, I think you had better decipher this code telegram and see if it is anything important." The code was Harry's only old-fashioned idiosyncracy carried over from earlier days. Otherwise, he remained a respected giant of the financial world, adapting to twentieth-century standards and increasing manyfold his share from the sale of Carnegie Steel.

With Jay proving that he was capable of running the business, Harry began setting up various trusts to distribute the majority of his remaining fortune to his five children. Previously, his only concern had been his children's ability to manage the tax-free fortune he had amassed, but now he also had to contend with new tax complications in distributing it. A long-term trust in the form of "joint ownership under common management" had been set up in 1907 when he turned over more than six million dollars of real estate holdings to his three sons. This format avoided taxation and accomplished his goal of providing for the future comfort of his family without the possible dissipation of capital by those less qualified in money matters than Jay.

In a letter to Jay, Hal, and Howard, written in Genoa, Italy, in 1907, Harry outlined his plans:

> My object is a double one in planning to turn over part of my estate to you. First—that I may be relieved of the great trouble at my time of life, and Second (which is more important) that you should each have something to work for, and I think the object will be accomplished, at least as a start, by presenting you with the properties mentioned hereafter.
>
> I think the properties should be managed as a whole instead of each one having his portion and having different management. How many years this joint ownership should last is a little difficult to say, but I think it should not be less than twelve or fifteen years, but I would lay down the rules upon which a division could take place so that there would be the minimum of trouble and unpleasantness.
>
> I would wish the earnings to accumulate till the end of the term, as you will each have sufficient income from other sources for all you will need. . . .
>
> It is my wish that one of you three should always be in America, or not have a longer interregnum than a month at most, as more than this would be too long a time without one of the owners being within reasonable call.

In 1911, Harry set up a larger trust along the same lines. The family holding company (known as Potomac Corporation, Bessemer Securities, and finally Bessemer Trust) had a corporate structure embracing countless subsidiaries organized for tax purposes. With an initial capitalization of approximately twenty million dollars in stocks, bonds, and real estate, the trust, under management known to the family simply as "The Office," dispersed its income to Harry's five children—Amy, Jay, Hal, Helen, and Howard—and their descendants. Originally, Harry had intended that each of them keep their own accounts rather than have his "business burdened with them." However, this arrangement proved unsuccessful, and subsequently the Office was made responsible for keeping the accounts of all members of the family as well as for processing all bills whether for purchases of property, payment of tradesmen and servants, charge accounts, or simply pocket money.

Although each of the five branches of the family was represented on the board of directors of the trust, the unquestioned overseer was Jay Phipps, who served as president and later chairman until his death in 1958. He ran the trust with an iron hand, never forgetting his father's words, "To him that hath, to him shall be given. If you take care of the money, you deserve to have it, not otherwise."

*Jay,* upper left, *and Hal,* lower right, *on trip to Yokahama*

*The dining room at 1063 Fifth Avenue, c. 1910*

# A HOME AT LAST

By 1901, Harry and Annie were ready to put their nomadic lifestyle behind them and move into a home of their own. In keeping with the prevalent mode of New York society, they commissioned an architectural firm—Trowbridge and Livingston—to build a New York City townhouse at Eighty-seventh Street and Fifth Avenue, just four blocks south of Andrew Carnegie's New York home. Their pseudo-classical marble mansion soon joined the rank of stately homes that marched along the greensward of Central Park from Fifty-ninth to Ninety-sixth Street, a stretch soon to be known as "Millionaire's Row."

Although as palatial and luxurious as any home on the row, their new townhouse did not suit them; Harry and Annie were simply not comfortable in such surroundings. It was pretentious, graceless, and cold, everything they were not. They were particularly unhappy about the interiors, and, the following summer, while at Knebworth, they leapt at the chance to voice their complaints to Amy's friend, George Crawley, an English designer who would soon be working on Jay's Long Island home, Westbury House. Harry was "very much pleased with Mr. Crawley on our visit to Liverpool," he wrote to Jay in November 1903, adding that Crawley "seemed very eager to get information and planning in a way that promises to be very advantageous." Crawley had agreed to come to New York the following year to finish the town-house. Later, with the work nearing completion, Harry remained enthusiastic about him, writing to Annie's brother, Harvey Shaffer, that "the new house looks first rate. . . . Crawley is really able in the line that Jay selected him for, and that is decoration."

With Annie, however, it was another story. She could not live with Crawley's expensive taste, and for his part, Crawley was upset by the difficulty in pleasing his client. In writing to Jay, Crawley accurately pin-pointed the problem and reasons for it:

> Your mother has decided not to have the bronze work done for the Library Mantlepiece, I regret to say. You saw and approved the design but she did not like it—the 2 tables for the breakfast room she saw & called them awful—she dislikes them so much that she will not have them sent over—*wh* is most unfortunate. Her own taste is for very simple & inexpensive

*Dining room fireplace detail—Atlas figures were sculpted by Frank Derwent Wood*

> things & the thought of what the cost of my various work has been preys upon her mind to such a degree that she simply loathes the sight of everything I have done great & small. She means to be very kind about it—but that is the plain fact. It seems a terrible pity that her wishes were not consulted more at the start—or in fact that I ever undertook the work but it can't be helped now. The total cost of all the work and

*The townhouse at 1063 Fifth Avenue*

*Annie, c. 1900*

*Harry, c. 1902*

*John Singer Sargent's portrait of Annie with her grandson, Winston Guest, 1906*

Opposite page: *Three generations, c. 1907:* from top, *Harry and Helen Phipps Martin holding her son, Townsend; Amy Phipps Guest holding her son, Winston; and Annie holding her grandsons, Bradley Martin,* left, *and Raymond Guest*

*A recording session at the Edison Studios, January, 1914:* seated left, *Harry Phipps and Andrew Carnegie with Edison personnel and technicians*

furniture & plate . . . has amounted to under $400,000 . . . I don't really think that very excessive for a white marble palace *wh* cost with its ground near 3 times that amount. Many people both in England & America have spent far larger sums in similar cases, I trust you will see this & later on endeavour to defend my work and reputation with your mother & father & tell them that I am not the awful monster of wasteful extravagance that they suppose & that many men of far less wealth have spent infinitely greater sums on their homes—*wh* is the simple truth.

Under the circumstances, it would have been almost impossible to please Annie. She simply was not comfortable in the opulence and superficial atmosphere of Millionaire's Row. And when the bills came in, Harry was none too pleased either. By then Crawley was at work on Westbury House, and in typical fashion, Harry wrote to Jay, "I understand that you have dismissed Crawley and I think every friend of yours will say you have done wisely." Dismissal of Crawley was wishful thinking on Harry's part, for Jay and Amy, Crawley's contemporaries and more

sophisticated than their parents, were completely in tune with his taste. After all, it had been Amy who had "insisted on using marble" for the townhouse, and Jay who had pronounced that the building "ought to be by far the best-looking house in New York," congratulating Amy on investing in marble. (Years later, in 1927, when the house at 1063 Fifth Avenue was demolished, Amy had the marble moved to her estate, Templeton, on Long Island, where to this day the great chunks of stone lie in a vacant field, a monument to a bygone era. At the same time, the Crawley-designed dining room, the finest room in the house, was moved intact and installed in a new wing of Jay's Westbury House.)

Annie and Harry kept up appearances, so important to Amy and Jay, by owning their marble mansion overlooking the park, but they spent little time there, preferring to travel and to visit their children and grandchildren. They also continued to keep pace with the fashions of the times in other ways, and, in 1907, Annie had her portrait painted by John Singer Sargent, whom Harry called "the Velasquez of the future." Harry, too, had his image captured for posterity. On February 7, 1914, he made what would be his next-to-last public appearance, when he

*Annie with her grandchildren,* from left, *Diana, Winston, and Raymond Guest, 1915*

*Harry visits the Phipps Conservatory in Pittsburgh to view the Chrysanthemum Show of 1915: his last public appearance.*

*Bonnie Blink, Harry and Annie Phipps' home in Great Neck, Long Island*

accompanied Andrew Carnegie to the Edison Studios in New Jersey where the two men had their voices and images recorded in a talking movie, a kinetoscope.

Soon afterward, Harry, age seventy-five, fell ill and for the next fifteen years was confined to bed most of the time. With her husband's health deteriorating, Annie was more than ready to leave Fifth Avenue once and for all. In 1916, she hired Horace Trumbauer, a Philadelphia architect, to build a plain, red-brick country house with white columns, a mansion by most standards, in Great Neck, Long Island, not far from the estates of their five children. Once Annie and Harry had moved into Bonnie Blink, as they christened their new home, the family visited often, looking in vain for signs of improvement in Harry's health. At the beginning, they seemed almost optimistic. On Good Friday, 1917, Amy wrote, "Darling Mother, I am so hoping dear Father is better—there is an answer to every problem if we only knew how to work it out." By 1920 hope was waning and Amy wrote in a letter to Jay, "Father keeps all about the same. No improvement."

Two years later, Annie and Harry marked their Golden Wedding Anniversary, a bittersweet occasion for Annie. Its poignancy was captured in this letter from a family friend:

> I have just learned that this is your golden wedding day! You will be living in happy memories of the past with your wonderful young husband of fifty years ago. How rare he has always been, my dear! So loving—so tender—so adoring. And what an interesting time you have spent together. Most people's lives are drab and empty in comparison.
>
> Travel and distinguished company. Sons and daughters who have always been a joy and pride to you both. Beautiful homes, freedom to go where you would and do as you wished and to gather about you all the lovely things your keen sense of the beautiful longed for.
>
> It is an Arabian Nights adventure! And through all the years to have as companion so rare a personality. What a joy! Even now when dear dear Mr. Phipps has lost the vigor of his prime and his mind is like "great bells jangled—out of time"—the bells are always great! The literary treasures with which his mind was filled in his youth are still there and come out of the shadows now and then! It is very beautiful—and touches one to the heart.

For the next eight years, Harry lay in bed quietly, reliving the years of travel, occasionally writing down a passage from literature or reciting a favorite poem. The family kept a close watch, their vigil ending only

*Annie's last public appearance—presenting the winner's trophy to her grandsons,* from left, *Raymond and Winston Guest and Michael Phipps, October 1934, Open Polo Championship, Meadow Brook Club*

with Harry's death in 1930. Annie's selflessness throughout the long ordeal had been complete, as a family friend, full of concern for her, noted to Jay, writing, "What a rare and beautiful devotion your darling mother has shown for [Harry] during the years of his illness. He was always a beloved presence in the house—we remember her for her gentle tender care of him. She will miss him. She will be lonely without him. Even though you all adore her, no one can ever take his place. He had become her little child."

Not long after Harry's death, Annie sold Bonnie Blink, saying that it "seemed too big with only myself to enjoy it." She moved to Knole, her daughter Helen Martin's Westbury estate, where she could be with her children and grandchildren in whom she delighted. On October 9, 1934, she attended the Open Polo Championship at the Meadow Brook Club and presented the winner's trophy to a four-member team that included three of her grandsons—Michael Phipps, and Raymond and Winston Guest. Less than two weeks later, she died.

*An aerial view of the Jay S. Phipps estate, Westbury, c. 1920, with Quaker farms on the outskirts*

# WESTBURY HOUSE

The wedding of Jay Phipps and Margarita Grace had taken place on November 11, 1903, at Battle Abbey, England, the home of the Grace family. After the ceremonies, Jay and Dita, as the bride was known, climbed into their large touring car and started off on a two-and-a-half-month honeymoon. Both were seasoned travelers, and they had decided upon a motor trip through India as a novel and adventurous honeymoon. They and their entourage of servants traveled in three cars specially outfitted with tent attachments to serve as sleeping quarters. They covered four thousand miles, bagged a tiger, rode elephants, visited Maharajas, and for the most part, stayed well off the beaten track. They marveled at exotic India, finding such sights as a moonlit tomb outside Umballa "over-awing, in fact uncanny," as Dita described it in an infrequent letter home. "We entered the tomb in the right spirit to appreciate the weirdness of this ancient burying place. The effect was most appalling, wild and eerie. Every word uttered echoed and re-echoed, while a continuous distant rumbling overhead kept one's nerves on jump." On another occasion, Dita noted India's reaction to their own passing procession: "The highway was swarming with travelers, on foot and riding on camels . . . and they all, camels and men and women and cattle, stared open-mouthed as we went by. The road was a delight and very smooth and well kept, and we autoed 123 miles in five hours and twenty seconds, stopping for hot lunch to be cooked." It was travel in the tradition of Harry Phipps.

Upon returning to New York, Jay resumed his duties in the Phipps office. Now a married man and soon to be a father, he was ready to settle into a home of his own. He had promised Dita that she would one day have an English country house and gardens reminiscent of those she had left at Battle Abbey, and he already had the perfect setting in mind for such a house. Some years before, in 1901, he had purchased a Quaker farm in Westbury, Long Island, where he stayed with friends while fox hunting and playing polo.

As early as 1877, the fox-hunting gentry from New York City had been using a small farmhouse just south of Westbury on the Hempstead Plains to kennel

*The original sketch by George Crawley for Westbury House's southeast chimney sundial, stone swag, and carvings. The inscription reads,* Ora Ne Te Rapiat Hora *(Pray That The Hour Is Not Stolen From You).*

*Honeymooning in India, 1903—Margarita ("Dita") Phipps née Grace on top of an elephant*

*Jay,* second from left, *with his trophy, India, 1903*

*Taking a fence, c. 1900*

*B. Winthrop, 1885*

*Thomas Hitchcock, Sr., on Trouble, 1883*

their hounds, and by 1881, they had incorporated into the Meadow Brook Hunt. At first they rented or bought small farmhouses nearby in which to spend the night during their weekends of sport in the country, but as the hunt became more popular, and polo, introduced from Newport, Rhode Island, in 1882, took hold on Long Island, they started to buy up neighboring farmland and to build more substantial homes. Westbury, just twenty miles from the city, with its heavily wooded, rolling hills interspersed by meadows and open fields was the perfect terrain for their sport.

For more than two centuries, Westbury had remained a secluded community of Quaker farms, isolated by choice from the world around it. When the gentry began arriving from the city, the Quakers were first amused by the newcomers' antics—chasing fox over stone walls and riding their horses helter skelter across the fields, even occasionally right through a farmer's garden. With little insight into the value of land other than for farming, the Quakers willingly sold their holdings at seemingly windfall profit prices, while the sporting gentry were pleased to be purchasing their recreational playground at the low price of farmland. Before long, the demography of Westbury had changed dramatically, and Quaker amusement had turned to bewilderment. In 1896, there had been some fifty Quaker farms occupying 90 percent of Westbury, and by 1903, only three remained. As early as 1900, at least one Quaker, Isaac Hicks, had seen the end of his way of life coming, and in a moving lament, he wrote, "How strange it seems that I am alone . . . and am like a bird sitting on a dead tree wondering where are all my associates . . . where are they now? A generation almost past and the young look with wonder at the old friend. Yes, the world around here moves rapidly. The great wealthy ones continually come and a large number of small ones too but our Friends, where are they . . . ¾ gone." Isaac Hicks died soon after writing this; by 1910, the change of lifestyle in Westbury was complete, and the days of self-sufficient Quaker farming were over.

Except for the eclectic architecture of the new estate owners' mansions, rising above the trees and

*Members of the Meadow Brook Hunt, 1886:* front row, from left, *Elliott Roosevelt, James F. D. Lanier, Thomas Hitchcock, Jr., Homer B. Richardson;* back row, from left, *Stanley Mortimer, Winfield S. Hoyt, Douglas Robinson, William K. Thorn, Jr., Adolph Ladenburg*

*The John D. Hicks farmhouse, Westbury, Long Island, c. 1900*

changing the skyline, the countryside remained as open as it had been during the Quaker years. Existing farm structures were adapted for estate use wherever possible and new stable complexes, polo fields, steeplechase courses, racetracks, tennis courts, golf courses, swimming pools and formal gardens were carefully assimilated within the vast landholdings of the estate, leaving the overall natural appearance of the land unchanged. Although the new owners took pride in the stately formality of their country houses and gardens, it had been the open fields and wooded hills that had first attracted them to Westbury, and

*Isaac Hicks, 1900*

From left, *Irene Catlin, Louise Wood, Dita Phipps, Amy Phipps, and Jay on the steps of the Hicks house porch, 1904*

this was to remain the same no matter how the lifestyle changed.

The new estates, like the farms they replaced, were largely self-sufficient—"from dairy farm to private polo field"—often employing upwards of a hundred workers. Once again these self-contained private domains allowed Westbury to withdraw from the outside world, isolating itself from the rapid growth in population and the urban expansion surrounding it. For almost the next forty years, Westbury was to remain a "world of its own."

In time all five children of Harry and Annie

Phipps owned estates in or near Westbury. Jay's initial land purchase consisted of 175 acres and the farmhouse that had once belonged to John D. Hicks, Isaac Hicks' father. Over the next thirty years, Jay purchased nine other adjacent farms, totaling several hundred additional acres. In one very un-Phipps-like "bargain," Jay, anxious to own a narrow strip of land for a right-of-way to a highway, agreed to the then exorbitant price of $1,400 an acre, demanded by a stubborn Quaker widow, Elizabeth Hiller. Even at that, she would only begin negotiations for the land after Jay had first purchased for $1,000 her aged and ailing

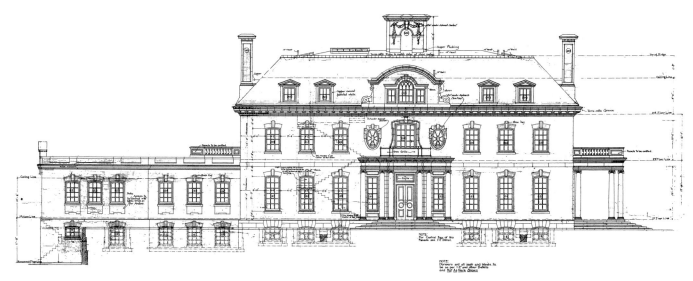

cow who grazed there. This he did, so determined was he to have the land.

Jay and Dita stayed at the Hicks homestead while they planned their own house and its gardens. Jay had recently become close friends with George Crawley, the thirty-nine-year-old London designer who had been commissioned by Jay's father to work on the interiors of the Fifth Avenue townhouse, and Jay now decided to hire him as architect of Westbury House. This was to be Crawley's first architectural project, and while he may have been lacking in experience, he had impeccable taste in all matters of design, a wide knowledge of English architectural detailing and styles, and, most importantly, a thorough understanding of his client's aspirations. For the next year, Crawley labored over his drawings, presenting them at last to Jay with the admonition, "I am certainly no genius and a good design does not come like Venus from the Sea but only with real labour and sorrow."

Jay was delighted by what he saw; Crawley had translated his client's wishes into a magnificent, perfectly proportioned country home in the style of Charles II. The cherry-red brick house with carved limestone detailing and a graduated Rutlandshire slate roof was sited high atop a hill just north of the old Hicks homestead, which would be moved once the building was completed. Laid out along an east-west axis and planned as an integral part of formal gardens and vistas, also designed by Crawley, the house faced out, both north and south, onto grand allées lined with beech and linden trees. On the outskirts of the

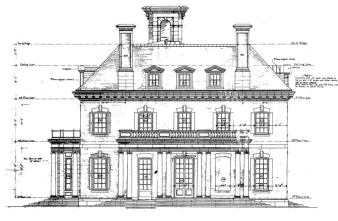

property, many of the old Quaker farmhouses were left nestled in acres of natural woods and open fields to act as counterpoints to the formality of the new estate.

Once Jay had approved the sketches, Crawley had a new challenge to face: the actual construction of his first architectural commission in a country far from his native England. To ease the process, Grosvenor Atterbury, the noted New York architect, was contracted to act as architect of record, drawing up the plans and specifications, all according to Crawley's designs. This seemingly ideal arrangement was

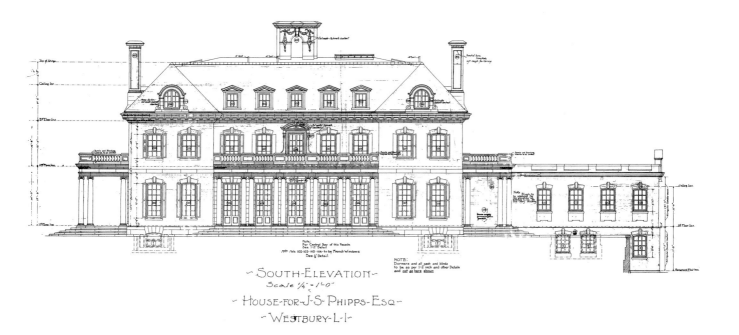

~SOUTH·ELEVATION~
Scale ¼" = 1'-0"
~House·for·J·S·Phipps·Esq~
~Westbury·L·I~

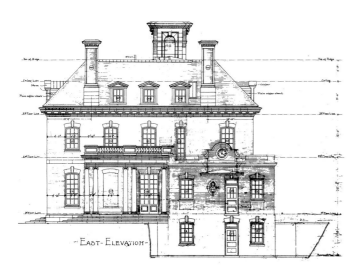

~East·Elevation~

fraught with conflict long before ground was even broken. Atterbury, more interested in structural innovation than aesthetics or historical detail, freely changed Crawley's designs to accommodate his own specifications, reducing the size of a window, for example, to make room for an important steel beam. At the same time, Crawley, the visionary, more interested in aesthetics than structural practicalities, rejected such alterations, insisting that the beam's location rather than the window be changed. He began to barrage Jay with letters complaining that Atterbury was tampering with the integrity of his design:

I have had three long days' work going over the last set of drawings sent by Atterbury and going into all the alterations made in them from my drawings which we had approved in Scotland. The list of alterations filled 6 or 7 pages of very close writing so I will not bore you giving every detail. . . . I have practically now changed everything back again to what we had previously agreed on and you will now get the house which we have all along contemplated and not a modern American adaptation of the same.

Recognizing his own inexperience and seeking to reassure Jay that the plans were "suitable to the best American practice," Crawley had them vetted for soundness by the general contractor Eidlitz who pronounced them, in Crawley's words, "quite practical and which if carried out make a building very different in feeling from Atterbury's interpretation of my ideas." Crawley knew however that Atterbury's expertise was essential to the project, and he ended his letter saying, "I trust as he [Atterbury] has been so sensible that we may be able to work smoothly together and that the result may be a success."

Unfortunately, Atterbury was not as cooperative as Crawley had hoped and, in Crawley's absence, continued to make substantial changes in the plans. Upon visiting Westbury, Crawley would discover the alterations, and finally, in exasperation, felt compelled to put the matter bluntly to Jay because he had "practically no choice . . . as it is quite obvious that if the

*Westbury House under construction, August 1905—the ground level has been raised on the south side in preparation for the terrace installation.*

*South side, November 2, 1905, complete except for the covering of Rutland roof tiles*

*North entrance, the front door, November 2, 1905*

*North side construction, 1905—the firebrick is piled up awaiting installation between the network of steel framing.*

house is to be a success it must be either Atterbury with a free hand or my design carried out as faithfully and accurately as possible. A perpetual compromise will only result in it not being either to his or to my taste."

There could be no question that Jay's taste was Crawley's taste and Jay lost no time in making it clear that Crawley was to design and Atterbury to construct adhering to Crawley's drawings, but both were to work harmoniously to this end. Jay's response to Crawley's letter—"I believe Gordon [of the Phipps office] knows that you have the authority to change Mr. Atterbury's plans as you wish but I will write to him to that effect again"—finally resolved the conflict once and for all.

During the three years that the house was under construction, 1904–1907, Jay and Crawley traveled back and forth between the United States and England, but rarely were the two of them on the building site at the same time to discuss plans and progress. They relied instead on a lengthy exchange of letters, photographs, and cables to resolve details and changes as the work progressed. Crawley, when he was not on hand, made sure that one of his two associates—Alfred C. Bossom (English) and Edward Hinkle (American)— was in Westbury to supervise, to "watch every brick laid." Crawley himself spent sleepless nights "thinking of it all. . . . I shall have put so much work into it and somehow things generally do go right in this world if you take unlimited trouble." Throughout the

job, Crawley "stoutly refused to see difficulties in either design or construction.'In architecture,' he used to say, 'I always believe in having my cake and eating it too,' and the result almost invariably was that some difficulty which had first appeared insurmountable to experts was finally overcome."[1]

His confidence in this ability to remove obstacles came to his aid on several occasions, as during a short-lived labor dispute over installation of the roof slate. The tiles had been imported from Rutlandshire, England, but when the English stone roofers from Colly-Weston arrived at Westbury on October 21, 1905, they were barred from working. Bossom explained to Jay in a November 11 letter that "unions here will not allow the men to handle work that has been previously handled by any other union, . . . even though they are all nominally receiving no pay (however an amount is being loaned to them each week apparently from myself)." Crawley, hearing of the difficulty, "was astonished to find that the 2 slaters had been kicking their heels doing nothing for more than 3 weeks. This was because everyone was afraid to take the responsibility of setting them to work in case of labour troubles. The law however undoubtedly permits the importation of labour to perform any work which cannot be performed in the country by American citizens—and as I knew that these men pos-

1. Cuthbert Headlam, *George Abraham Crawley: A Short Memoir* (London; privately printed, 1929).

*Hicks Nurseries transplants a mature beech tree to a site outside the west porch as the house nears completion in 1906.*

*Work progresses on the cornice and bricks, east side, July 20, 1905*

*The west porch, September 1907*

sessed the only set of tools in the country to work this slate, I decided at once to take the responsibility myself and start them to work which I did and I trust I shant be landed in jail."

On only one occasion did Phipps and Crawley openly disagree and that was over the terrace on the south side of the house. Work had commenced on it in October 1905 and, as Bossom wrote to Phipps, was "proceeding with great rapidity. The rear wall of concrete is slowly rising up in form, and the foundations of the front wall are all in now, practically from the middle of the foundations of the house to the west end. All the excavation to bring the ground to the general court level from this point toward the east is also completed."

However, when the cost estimates came in for the terrace's brick wall, limestone stairway, and upper balustrade, Phipps became concerned and started to whittle away at Crawley's elaborate design, eliminating decorative piers and niches, and substituting terra cotta for limestone. Crawley was unhappy with his client's changes and defended the designs and their cost on aesthetic grounds, explaining that "if the design is pulled to pieces and has all the interesting features cut out of it, it will look altogether an inadequate setting to the house itself, and I should rather have had an entirely different set of designs."

Jay too used aesthetics as his excuse for making changes, quickly reassuring Crawley that "regarding your design, I certainly do not wish it pulled to pieces. I have marked out the stone blocks in the pilasters along the wall, and in the picture the effect was certainly improved. However, after carefully studying the question, if you feel positive you prefer the stone blocks, you may put them in. My reason for omitting these blocks was not to save cost in construction but simply because I thought the effect would be im-

proved, but in regard to this I leave the matter entirely to you to do as you think best."

Jay was not being completely truthful about costs, nor was he able to let the matter rest, for a week later he wrote a very strong letter, cutting the heart out of Crawley's design on a basis of cost alone:

G.A.C., Esq., NY, 7/12/05
I was at Battle shooting from Friday until Tuesday, and there received your letter urging that the stone blocks should be built in the pilasters of the Westbury Garden terrace and I cabled—"Crawley decide balustrade and details terrace including stone blocks in pilasters."

On my arrival in London I had a big mail from Tommy Moore, Gordon, you and others. After reading Eidlitz's estimate for the garden terrace I came to the conclusion that however fine it might look I was unwilling to spend so much money on the place. As you know his estimate is that the cost will be $44,000, not counting the cost of the small 4' wall back of the main terrace, and Moore writes that the final cost will certainly approach $50,000.

I am very disappointed, and regret so much time has been wasted. I have an idea that all having anything to do with my house in New York have acquired a notion that nothing is too good for it, and "damn the expense." What I

*After completion of the house, work continued in the formal gardens—here the treillage in the Walled Garden begins to take shape.*

want and what I have always asked for is an inexpensive country home, and I think it is ridiculous to run into so much money as your present plan would cost if carried out. I have therefore cabled:—"Crawley stop terrace after finishing concrete construction. Must change design limiting cost $20,000. Writing. Night-hawk."

I believe a terracotta balustrade will be plenty good enough, and with several changes we will be more than able to reduce the cost of the terrace by half. I certainly do not want a stone walk ten feet wide between the low wall and the balustrade of the main terrace; that is to be a gravel walk. I do not want the circular niches in the wall made of stone; they could have a white stone bracket at the base, but must not be lined and made entirely of stone.

After the constructional part of my terrace is finished, before proceeding, let me see sketches and estimates for the finished cost.
Sincerely,
JSP

Unknown to Crawley, much of Jay's reaction was prompted by his parents' dismay over the cost of the work Crawley had done on their Fifth Avenue townhouse. At the time, Harry had written Jay about his unhappiness with Crawley's extravagance warning that terraces and lawns were expensive to maintain; Jay must have been somewhat shaken by his father's ending the letter with the reminder that "you are spending money you have not yet earned." In any event, for the time being, all work was stopped on the terrace, and Crawley went back to the drawing board with a new imperative: "prepare something less ambitious and keep cost as low as possible, of course having due regard to the effect."

Somehow, eight months later, in a dramatic reversal Jay permitted Crawley to go ahead with the original terrace design. Crawley had spent the winter and spring convincing Jay that he was only doing what he had been commissioned to do, that "no one could be keener or more interested than I am and you may rest assured that I shall not spare myself in any way to make everything successful so that the large outlay you are making may be fully justified by the result."

In August, 1906, work was resumed, and by September, Crawley reported that he had "been to Westbury today. The place shows some progress and the terrace is getting on. One of the oval niches is in place with its brackets which looks A-1. I am sure you will like it." A month later, he assured Jay that he would "be pleased with the terrace. I can say no more than that. I think the result justifies the expenditure upon it."

*View of the terrace, summer 1906, completed as Crawley had en*

*windmill supplied water during construction.*

Above: *The entrance hall, like all of Westbury House, was
designed and furnished by George Crawley*
Right: Portrait of George Crawley *by Oswald Birley, 1919*

Previous page: *The first floor study, another reflection of the
taste and care which Crawley employed in the interior design
of Westbury House*

*Inscription and carving over the front door, Crawley's finishing touch to his first major architectural project*

Westbury House, its interiors, and formal gardens were all designed and contructed simultaneously as a unified whole; Crawley could as easily be found on the grounds laying out the Rose or Walled Gardens as inside the house supervising the execution of a ceiling mural or placement of an armoire he had purchased for Jay. During the years of construction, Crawley had carefully searched out appropriate antique furnishings for the interior of the house. He would write to Jay describing his findings and, after getting initial approval, would gather the pieces together for Jay's final inspection. In one case, he wrote from Paris, "I have just been to see old Rodin and he has lots of interesting things in hand . . . shall be in London Tuesday—I think it will be best if you come to town on Thursday or Friday so that I can have 2 days to have everything ready for your inspection." When Crawley could not find a suitable antique for a certain setting, he would replicate what he envisioned, using the finest craftsmen in Europe. Whether a door lock, silver chandelier, or marble mantlepiece, it had to be just right to meet with Crawley's approval.

While Jay for the most part relied on Crawley's judgment in these matters, his own taste and confidence in choosing antiques was growing, being shaped by these acquisitions. Often Crawley had to use tact to restrain his client's enthusiasm, which led him to buy more than was needed. On one such occasion, Crawley wrote to Jay, "I can't use any more Chinese paper; . . . two rooms are quite enough at Westbury—more will overdo it—you see you can't hang pictures or prints on them." Even after com-

pletion of Westbury House, Jay still depended on Crawley's judgment in selecting antiques and insisted upon paying him a 5 percent commission on their purchases, saying, "it will make me feel more at liberty to ask you to select things for me and I consider myself very lucky to have the benefit of your advice on that basis."

By the early spring of 1907, the house lacked only a front door; on the first of March, Crawley wrote to Jay, "I have got the front door underway at last. It has given me more trouble than anything I have ever done. I think I have made it 50 times without ever being satisfied. I wanted a very fine door which was completely out of the ordinary with lots of character. It was of course always open to me to do the simple commonplace thing but I would not give it up. Yesterday morning, it all came right, the very thing I desired and if I tried ten years I could not do anything better. I hope and believe you will like it. I am completely happy about it. You may have thought of me as very lazy but it baffled me and has been on my mind for two years."

Jay approved fully of the new door, and his family, which now included two sons, Ben and Hubert, and a baby daughter, Peggie—born November 17, 1906—was ready to move into their new home. In May 1907, they passed beneath the portals of Crawley's "very fine door," over which is inscribed:

*Pax Introentibus—Salus Exeuntibus*
("Peace to Those Who Enter—Good Health to Those Who Depart").

*Peggie  Phipps, Westbury, 1916*

# II. Memories

The following chapters are the story of Westbury House during its short life of fifty years while it was a home and a warm and pleasant dwelling place filled with happiness, sorrow, and lots of laughter. I have tried to sketch in the family that lived there, and friends and relatives who visited, and the people who worked in the house.

My recollections encompass four generations including my grandparents, mother and father, their children, and grandchildren. My granddaughter, the third Dita, was the only great-grandchild born while the house was still lived in.

Most of my memories are seen through the eyes of a child, for it was during the first quarter of this century, while we were all at home, that Westbury House and its gardens were the focal point of our lives. Through all those years, nothing momentous or extraordinary ever deeply touched Westbury. I have no tales to tell of changing fortunes, catastrophes or scandals, or even great triumphs. Nonetheless, I hope that the peaceful years and even tenor of its ways have marked Westbury House and the Gardens as I believe they are—a precious rarity in this changing world.

Peggie Phipps Boegner

*John Shaffer ("Jay") Phipps*

# FATHER

Father had a many-sided character, though he was usually described as a sportsman and financier; he was also a devoted family man, a collector of rare, beautiful things, and a lover of the land. He had an eye for land both as a business venture and a cherished place where you lived, put down family roots, and planted trees. He and Mother had a mutual passion for building houses and gardens. They had six houses, each one very different but all attractive and well suited to their surroundings. While not a serious connoisseur, Father was able to select beautiful furniture and paintings. Among his most valuable acquisitions were two violins—a Stradivarius and a Quanavarius—which he kept in a hidden closet in Mother's study. From time to time, he would bring them out—to admire them and to play a few bars of *Humoresque* by Dvořák.

Considering how religious Grandma Phipps and Aunt Amy were, it was rather surprising that our family had no formal religion. We considered ourselves Protestants in a rather vague way—naturally, we did not say grace before meals, but Father sometimes quoted his favorite grace by Robert Burns: "Some hae meat and canna eat, and some wad eat that want it, but we hae meat and we can eat, and sae the Lord we thanket." Perhaps Father had a slightly guilty feeling of having so much, or perhaps he just liked Robert Burns.

From an early age, Father took his position as head of the Phipps family very seriously. In business, his great interest was real estate. Both he and his elder sister, Amy Guest, seemed to have had a real flare and imagination for investing in land. Among their most successful ventures were their purchases through the Phipps office of the slumlike areas around Fifty-seventh Street and the East River—now Sutton Place—of vast tracts of land in Florida, Miami, and Palm Beach, of waterfront in Barnegat Bay in New Jersey, and stretches of marsh and forest land in the Hamptons on Long Island.

I don't remember Father going to New York for business every day, though I suppose he did when we were small. I picture him sitting in an armchair in his study, his hunting dog beside him, holding a nonstop telephone conversation with the office or the stables, the *Times* and the racing sheet on the floor. He never

*Jay with his friend Dudley Carlton at Newport, Rhode Island, 1907*

retired for he could not bear to relinquish his unquestioned authority.

As Mother and Father had completely adopted each other's families, they really had little need for friends who were not relatives. Father was very fond of Jasha Hamburg, an exuberant Russian Jewish violinist, who often stayed at Westbury and gave Ben violin lessons. Mr. Hamburg played really beautifully on Father's violins. His brother, Marc Hamburg, was a well-known pianist, and another brother, Boris, played the cello.

Mr. Hamburg also gave me lessons, but only for

*Jay with his oldest child, Ben, at Battle Abbey, England, 1907*

a short time as a punishment for my not practicing the piano. We were mutually relieved when I was handed back to my lovely red-haired piano teacher, Miss Spence, who at one time had been an accompanist for Fritz Kreisler. Now, whenever I see a Marc Chagall painting, I think, "There goes old Jasha floating around with his fiddle."

Viscount Cowdray was a polo-playing friend; his background must have been much like Father's as the eldest son of the founder of a fortune. They both enjoyed their wealth tremendously, and while working hard at business, they had plenty of time to spend their money on such satisfying things as beautiful

houses, gardens, horses, cars, shooting lodges, and the extravagant rearing of their large families.

Lord and Lady Cowdray plus two or three children sometimes stayed with us in Palm Beach or in Westbury for the international polo matches. We only visited them once. While I was at Oxford with my friend Betty Sharp, Father drove us to Midhurst, the Cowdray's very baronial hall. I was fond of John Cowdray, who was at Oxford with us, and of Yoskil, the oldest daughter (named after her father's favorite polo pony), and of the rest of the family, but the size of the castle and the number of clip young guardsmen and innumerable footmen and other servants hovering

*Resting between chukkers, 1931*

*The "Freebooters" team at the Cathedral Fund charity match, Westbury, 1925: from left,* Dev Milburn, Bobby Strawbridge, Tommy Hitchcock, and Jay Phipps

over us awed us. Our first evening, Betty and I clung to Father as a port in the storm, but when we came down next morning dressed for the hunt, we learned that he had already departed for London, leaving us to manage quite successfully for ourselves.

George Crawley was another close friend; he was a great connoisseur of eighteenth-century art and architecture. During the many years of designing Westbury Gardens, building the house, and buying the furniture and paintings for it, he was constantly with us, sometimes accompanied by his charming wife, a friend of Mother.

And then there was Uncle Malcolm Chace and his family. It was customary in those days for the children to call the family's close friends "aunt" or "uncle." Uncle Malcolm and Father first met when they were both freshmen at Yale. Uncle Malcolm's story is that he looked out the window of his room one day about a week after college opened and saw

Father arriving, wearing a bowler hat and carrying a canary in a cage. They soon became great friends, and this affectionate relationship has carried on through three generations. In fact, the Chaces were the only outside family that we knew well and ranked with our cousins. Uncle Malcolm was boisterous, friendly, a complete extrovert, and a typical American.

With Father's upbringing divided between Europe and the United States and no permanent home until he married and settled down in Westbury, you could hardly say he was typical of anything—each of these four friends satisfied one side of his character.

As I don't really feel that I knew Father as intimately as I did the rest of the family, I have asked about him from some of his contemporaries. They were all fond of him and found him charming, intelligent, rather shy, and highly strung. I think they also agreed that it was lucky that he chose Mother to be his lifelong companion. Mrs. Fred Allen, a close family friend, told her daughter, "All the girls were after Jay. He was so charming and attractive and, of course, a great catch—and then he married a simple English girl with a will of iron." Mother was not simple at all, but she was innocent and unworldly, and she knew exactly what was right.

In the days of my childhood, fathers did not play the important part in bringing up their children that they now do. Even though Father was the titular head of the family, if we wanted permission for anything, we would go to Mother. If it was the other way around, he would inevitably say, "Ask your mother" or "I don't think you should do it, it might worry your mother." Father was innately shy, and though he was fond of all his children, he was only close to Michael whom he adored.

It was in the world of books and hunting that Father and I enjoyed each other's company, and we spent many happy hours hunting together in Virginia, on Long Island, and, during one short season, with the Bicester hunt near Oxford. In his time, Father was a six-goal polo player. He also was a good rider in a rather energetic way. Whenever we were all gathered round to go hunting or hacking, he would suddenly dig his heels into his horse, and with a whoop, they would be off, scattering everyone in all directions. The boys thought this amusing, but I tried hard to keep my pony's head pointed in a different direction until calm was restored.

Father had read a lot in his youth. He seems to have had the same natural taste in literature that he showed in furniture, art, and architecture. It was he who introduced me to his favorite classics, and they became mine also; Milton, Shelley, and Keats headed the list. I was well paid to learn their poems by heart. I am grateful for this, for they have lived on in my memory and have colored my life with beauty and fantasy. Then there was Grey's *Elegy in a Country Churchyard,* the Brownings, Byron, Swinburne, and Rupert Brooks. In prose I read all of Scott, Meredith, Hardy, Dickens, and Trollope. I still read Jane Austen when I have a cold. What a charming, wonderful world of books for a young person to enjoy.

Being paid to learn poetry makes me think of Uncle Malcolm again, whose children and grandchildren were given twenty dollars to learn the Declaration of Independence. Father's and Uncle Malcolm's choice of what to pass on to their children is indicative of the two characters.

Father also enjoyed getting off a few shady remarks from time to time, which we all thought very funny. Mother would pretend to be shocked and say in her best Victorian manner, "We are not amused." Mother, however, truly disapproved of Uncle Freddy Guest and Uncle Malcolm who, she thought, were

*Jay on the Westbury courts*

bad influences on Father—especially since their jokes and very moderate drinking could not be curbed by their wives.

One year Father and Uncle Malcolm planned to go to England and France, sailing on the *Mauritania.* We all went down to the pier to see them off. When we got to the cabins, Uncle Malcolm said, "Jay, I don't see your luggage." "No," said Father. "I decided that

*Captain John S. Phipps, 1917*

*Jay,* far left, *with members of his squadron, 1917*

I didn't really want to leave Dita, but you go on and have a good trip—bon voyage." One had to accept the fact that Father was unpredictable.

During the 1918 war, Father was a captain and then a major in the ground aviation. First he went to Plattsburg, New York, for his military training, and then he was stationed at Mitchell Field in Mineola where he could live at home. I'm sure he was an efficient officer, but I wonder how he fitted into army protocol. One day when he had invited his commanding officer and another bigwig to lunch, he got up in the middle of the meal and said that he had to go to the stable to see his horses. Though I was pretty young at the time, I remember the feeling of shock and surprise that rippled around the table.

Later, he went to Fort Worth, Texas, with Major C. K. Rhinehardt and was just about to be sent overseas when the war ended. It was during this time that I remember Father telling us about the following episode, saying that he was absolutely terrified. The newspaper headline read, "Flier Returns After Narrow Escape on Trip," and the story reported that "Capt. J. Phipps of the American Corps, Taliaferro field, has returned from San Antonio where he landed Thursday night after an arduous flight in company with Maj. C. K. Rhinehardt. Reports from San Antonio say that the two flying

officers were 3,000 feet in the air when a wing of the plane was broken. Captain Phipps took the wheel and Major Rhinehardt replaced the missing wing with his own body. The accident occurred about sixty miles from San Antonio. In this crippled condition the officers effected a landing about 6 o'clock p.m. Thursday."

Though Father always had hunters and polo ponies, he became interested in racing through the good offices of his brother, Hal Phipps. When Father was about sixty-seven, he had a slight heart attack. Our doctor told Uncle Hal that he thought it was dangerous for his brother to watch the polo matches in which Michael played. If Michael had a fall or if it even looked as though there might be an accident, Father could have another attack. If only he could be persuaded to have racehorses, they would give him the thrill of a polo match minus the anxiety over Michael. So Uncle Hal presented me with one of his extra racehorses, a grey mare called DuBarry. We all went together to Belmont Park to see her run. She won her race—she never did again, but the plan had succeeded. Soon after, Father started his racing stable, which kept him happy and was great fun for the rest of the family with the exception of Mother. Though Mother was a good rider and had hunted a lot in England and America, she didn't approve of the racing

*Greeting his springer spaniel at Westbury House, 1940*

*Heading for the winner's circle, Belmont Park, 1953*

set. Father and my brother Hubert were drawn to "characters," and there are always plenty of them around the track.

A peculiarity of Father's, which amused him but sometimes caused some consternation among his friends, was his habit of making faux pas. I remember one day in Palm Beach Mother was giving a luncheon party for the people who had entertained Uncle Josh Benskin and Aunt Gladys, Mother's sister, during their winter visit. Father was not there. At an interesting moment when Ben was explaining to the guests just how a skunk could be an excellent pet if it was properly deskunked, Father came into the dining room,

smiled graciously at the guests, walked around the table, and putting his arm around Mother, said, "Dita, guess what? I went to Amy's to avoid our luncheon party and got roped into a large party at her house and couldn't leave."

Like many men of that time, when Father was older he became restless and traveled a lot, taking short journeys to his properties in Florida—in Palm Beach and Tallahassee—Virginia, or Cape Cod. If Mother didn't go with him, he was apt to come home a day or two earlier than expected as a pleasant surprise for his wife, for with all his restless energy Father really did love to be home.

*Christmas at Westbury House, 1936—Jay pours brandy on the plum pudding.*

*Margarita Cecilia ("Dita") Grace upon her presentation at the Court of Queen Victoria, 1894*

# MOTHER

My mother, Margarita Cecilia Grace Phipps, mistress of Westbury House, was born in Lima, Peru, October 31, 1876. When she was fourteen, the family moved to New York, and three years later, they moved to London. She lived in England until 1903 when she married and came with her husband to Long Island, where she spent the rest of her life.

The whole of Westbury House revolved around Mother, who had such a store of affection and delight for each and every member of her family that, like a magnet, she drew all of us into her orbit. Our house was also the gathering place for the uncles, aunts, and cousins—both Phippses and Graces. Father and Mother were "Uncle Jay" and "Aunt Dita" to a host of young people.

Mother had that wonderful faculty of seeing no wrong in those she loved. This gift seemed to be quite common among Edwardian ladies. Nowadays, we look at people objectively which perhaps is a good thing, but it lacks the charm and comfort of knowing that at least to someone you are beyond criticism.

All of Mother's interests were centered on her immediate family. She never spoke of politics and only voted once in her lifetime; even then she pulled the wrong lever and cast her vote for Debs, the Socialist candidate. She hadn't the vaguest idea about money. She had plenty from her father, but she had been brought up with the attitude that anything to do with finances was her husband's affair. When Mother's youngest sister, Gladys, became a widow during the 1914 war, she asked their father how much income she had so that she could plan her budget accordingly. He answered, "Don't worry your head about that. Spend whatever you want and if you are overdrawn, I will let you know." Reluctantly she agreed to this plan mainly because, in those days, it was considered vulgar for a lady to talk about finances. So Mother too just put money matters out of her mind. Only once did I see her annoyed with Father for spending her money without asking her. One afternoon at teatime, Father announced casually that he had just bought a fifty-thousand-dollar mare at her expense. She was quite shocked. In the first place, she didn't like the idea of racing because of the betting, and then too it did seem a rather large sum of money for a mare. She tried to pretend that it was a stallion

*Dita, age five, Lima, Peru*

and therefore a good business deal, but we all kindly said, "Oh, no, Mother, it is a mare."

With her upbringing, it would have been astounding had Mother ever interested herself in the stock market or even in her will. However, she had an innate knowledge of the human character, and she managed Father, her four children, and six houses with the greatest of ease. Wherever we went, there were always plenty of servants, food, freshly made beds, flowers in vases, visitors, and a feeling of home.

I suppose she and Father spoiled us in many ways, though there were a few rules that we were not allowed to break. We could not tell a lie, cheat at games, swear, or tell vulgar stories; and if we were hurt, we were supposed to be brave. I can remember staying in my bedroom for a day because I said "damn you, damn you" to my governess, hoping that I was sending her straight to hell.

When Ethel M. Dell's book, *The Sheik of Araby*, came out, one of my male cousins slipped it to me, and I read it late at night, by flashlight. When it was made into a movie, half of our class at Miss Chapin's planned to meet secretly one afternoon to go see it. This scheme involved a certain amount of prevarication and double talk. My conscience would not let me go along with it, so I told Mother our plan. At the time, we were living with Grandma Phipps in her house on Fifth Avenue, so the next day, Mother and Grandma went off to see the movie—and I'm sure they

*Dita and her cousin, Joseph P. Grace, 1882*

*"The Three Graces"*—from left, *Dita, Elisa, and Elena*

112

*Dita, a bridesmaid at Elisa Grace's wedding to Hubert Beaumont, 1892*

enjoyed it immensely, for a few days later, Father was delegated to take two honest but embarrassed little girls to see *The Sheik*. Poor Father; my friend, in a very obvious manner, put her head in her lap during the "bad" parts and squealed during others where she thought it appropriate.

When the boys were at college and later when one by one we children were young marrieds, we would bring our weekend guests to Sunday lunch at the family's. Suffering a bit from the Saturday night parties, some of the guests would have a drink before arriving for the delicious but alcohol-less luncheon. Years later, one of Ben's old college friends said to me, "You know, there was something that astonished me at your family's Sunday lunches. Mrs. Phipps was the most ladylike person I have ever met, yet sometimes when one of us would forget where he was and tell a definitely 'shady' story, she would laugh and giggle with all the rest of us. It seemed so out of character." "No," I explained, "it was just that she thought you were telling a 'shaggy dog' story or a pointless joke. Of course to her they were pointless and ridiculously funny as she couldn't see the point." In this second half of the century, it is difficult to realize the strong Victorian influence that still existed in the early 1900s.

Though I was so fond of my mother and lived near her for fifty years, first at home, then next door where I moved after my marriage, my knowledge of her life is rather sparse. For one thing, she was extremely reticent about her personal affairs and was careful not to gossip about other people's private lives. All her emotions were very controlled. In later life, she was a benevolent matriarch—surely the best sort of government that there is for a family or a country.

So that is the way I remember her, dressed in some soft color, plump and pretty as a picture, presiding over the tea table with children and friends and grandchildren around, the inevitable dachshunds at her feet.

Last year we discovered some of her early letters to Father hidden away in a closet. On reading them, it became apparent that she had been a most innocent, loving young person and in some ways quite unsure of herself. She was content with the life she led at home with her sisters. It must have been very pleasant. None of them married until they were in their late twenties. In my Aunt Glad's diary, there were so many cousins one wonders how the girls ever found suitable husbands. In those days, people were less nervous. They ate a lot, slept well, and enjoyed their social life and sports; they read novels, played the piano, and laughed over silly little jokes. The magazine *Punch* typified the humor of that era. Rather

*Dita with her children:* from left, *Ben, Peggie, Michael, and H*

115

*Phipps children with their wartime guests from England, 1941*

surprisingly, the letters frequently mentioned headaches and indigestion, both, I suppose, because they ate too much.

Once Mother told me a story, perhaps for its built-in moral or else just as a bit of nostalgia for the good old days. One afternoon when she was playing the piano, a beau stole up behind her and kissed her neck. She rose and rang the bell for a footman. When he came, she told him "James, Mr.——— is leaving. Please show him out."

Father told me that one evening he went to a ball in London, and when he came home he woke his brother Howard and said, "I have just seen the girl whom I am going to marry." This proved to be true. Mother and Helen Phipps, Father's sister, met while they were both doing the London season, and they became great friends. Subsequently, there was much visiting between the Phippses and the Graces. Mother often stayed at Beaufort Castle in Invernesshire, a shooting place that Grandpa Phipps rented for several summers.

Father and Uncle Hal invented a game called "Ride a Cock Horse." The girls would start cantering across the moors on their Hill ponies, and the young men would gallop madly after them, seize them by the waist, and pull them onto their ponies in the

manner of the Wild West movies. Mother said it was very exciting. Father agreed, adding, "It was the only time I could get my arms around your mother without her pushing me away."

Mother was staying with Aunt Helen in Scotland when Father proposed. She answered that she wasn't sure that she wanted to get married, and he sank to his knees in the soggy bog where they were standing and said, "I won't get up until you have accepted me." And, as always, Mother accepted anything that Father asked. When Father and Mother finally decided to announce their engagement, they drove up to Beaufort Castle. The whole Phipps family was gathered on the front steps to greet them. Mother was seized by a sudden panic of shyness. She begged Father to stop, jumped out of the car, ran around the house and up the back stairs. She is referring to this incident in a charming letter which she later wrote from Battle Abbey. "All the family—Aunts, Uncles, and Cousins—will be here to meet my wonderful husband-to-be. Jay Bird, you will have to be brave—there are no back stairs at Battle Abbey."

Their marriage was a long and beautiful relationship with a great deal of love and admiration on both sides and, I have to admit, a lot of patience on my mother's part.

*In the White Drawing Room at Westbury House, 1940: Peggie,* right, *holding dachshund Peter; Dita,* center, *holding Tiny and Happy; and Dita Douglas holding Teefy; Chewie the pit bull sits in the foreground.*

*John H. H. ("Ben") Phipps, 1921*

# BEN

It is much harder to portray those nearest and dearest to us than to write a description of an aunt or a grandparent. Of my relations, I have a picture, or perhaps a caricature, neatly drawn in my memory; but for my three brothers, with whom I spent my whole childhood and youth, it is more complicated. There were four of us, and, as there were only six years between the oldest and the youngest, we had a wonderful time together.

Ben was the oldest son of the oldest son, and the first of the third generation of Phipps. He was quickly followed by a slew of siblings and cousins, both American and English. In Westbury alone, there were fifteen of us (not counting Uncle Howard's two children who arrived many years later), and there were five in England.

Ben was born in an attractive house in London, rented especially for his arrival. It was supposed to be haunted. His nurse swore that she had seen a lady in gray lean over his crib weeping. When the nurse approached, the lady disappeared. This happened several times. The poor lady must have been weeping for her own sorrows because it had no effect on Ben who was rather lucky throughout his life.

His given name was John Henry Howard, but he was always called Ben, a name that suited him very well. The reason for this nickname came about because Mother and Father were staying in Scotland the summer of 1904; and, as Mother was very large, the child-to-be was referred to as Ben, after the nearby mountain, Ben Nevis. Mother used to drive around in a bath chair pulled by two donkeys. One day they ran away and nearly dumped her. Everyone was terrified for the unborn baby but all was well, and Ben arrived on time, a beautiful, healthy child.

He was a natural leader. He protected me, looked after Hubert, and taught us all natural history and Indian lore. Like all children of that generation who lived in the country, we spent most of our time playing in the garden. Our games in Westbury Gardens were taken from the books we read and the few movies we saw, and it was Ben who invented the games and made the rules—Indians and big-game hunters were our favorites. We were not keen to share our games with outsiders, so when Mother invited some of her friends' children to tea, we would play

*Dita and Ben, 1904*

hide and seek and successfully hide in some appointed place until after teatime when the guests had to leave.

Winston, Raymond, and Diana Guest, Aunt Amy's children, often stayed with us; the two families and the other cousins of our age, Bradley and Townsend Martin, and Ogden and Bobbi Phipps, made up a full tribe of Mohicans. In the fall, our weapons were not bows and arrows but small green apples which we

Above: *Ben,* left, *and Tommy Hitchcock, Jr., at the Piping Rock Club, 1911.* Right: *Ben, Westbury, 1909.*

Previous page: *Michael Paul Grace,* far left, *and his daughter Dita who sits in the cart that overturned, Battle Abbey, England, 1903*

*Ben in a quiet pose, Westbury, 1910*

Above: *With a friend at Palm Beach, c. 1916—years later Ben became president of the Conservation Corporation to Save the Green Turtle.*
Right: *Golfing at Palm Beach, 1916*

would throw at our enemies. We tried to hit the mark but not too hard, as an unripe apple can be quite a painful missile. During the summer months, we would silently steal through the gardens from tree to tree, walking with our toes turned in, Indian style. Occasionally, we would put our ears to the ground to listen for an approaching enemy.

I remember one afternoon when I had safely reached the terrace above the orchard and could spy over all the garden. I saw Winston and Raymond creeping around the hedge, fairly well hidden until they bent over and put their ears to the ground to listen (for footsteps). They had forgotten that their mother had bought them both elegant, shrimp-pink linen trousers from Swears & Wells on Bond Street. They could be seen for miles away. They were ashamed of their pink pants, but in those days, you wore what your parents chose for you. I remember Ben had a brown velvet suit with short trousers and an ecru-colored lace jabot. He looked too lovely, but he was miserable and fought hard to avoid going to dancing class in it. My best dress was made of Irish lace with a large pink sash around the middle. Every little em-

Above: *Giving Roswald a ride in a motorized Redbug, Palm Beach, 1918*
Left: *Shooting in Florida, 1915*

broidered rose tickled or scratched, and I didn't think I looked my best in it anyhow.

When Ben was fourteen, he was sent to Groton School in Massachusetts. It was an unfortunate choice. Though an excellent school scholastically, it was both strict and snobbish, closely following the English Public School tradition. Coming from a loving and admiring family, to Ben it was quite a shock. His marks were not good; and when he brought a skunk into Chapel one Sunday, the famous Dr. Peabody suggested that he finish his education somewhere else.

He then went to Exeter, also in Massachusetts, and from there, to Yale. On graduation in June 1928, he married Eleanor Klapp ("Klippy"), and they spent their honeymoon in Kenya. This was long before the time of conducted African safaris and planes. On one of the trips, they brought back to camp a twenty-foot python, with six of them carrying it through the jungle, and Klippy wrote to me; "I wish you could see Percy the Python go for a walk with Ben. It's disgusting. He goes tearing along with his collar and chain on, through the grass, or makes ugly snaps at Ben who wards him off with a stick." In a letter to

*On the north lawn, before the newly planted beech allée,
Westbury House, c. 1913:* from left, *Winston and Diana
Guest, Peggie Phipps, Eliot Chace, Ben Phipps, Raymond
Guest* (astride), *Malcolm Chace, Hubert Phipps, Michael
Phipps* (astride), *a stable lad, Lillias Kent, and a governess*

*Aunt Helen Phipps Martin with her sons, Bradley,* left, *and Townsend, in their blue satin outfits, Christmas, c. 1914*

*Diana Guest, c. 1914*

*Raymond Guest, c. 1914*

Michael, Ben wrote that he and Klippy wanted to stay on in Africa and buy a coffee plantation. "We would settle here in a minute if it was not for the family. We miss you all as much as you miss us," he wrote.

They loved this wild country and planned to live there, but had to change their minds after their sons were born, so they bought thirteen thousand acres of land near Tallahassee, Florida. Their house overlooks Lake Jackson, and, with the rolling countryside and giant live oaks, one could easily imagine oneself in Kenya.

Ben was a colonel during the Second World War. On his return to Tallahassee, he bought a television station and also became director of various companies connected with the family business. He was one of the first ranchers to realize the importance of Florida as a cattle state, and he introduced the white Charolais into this country. He organized a group to save the green turtle and their laying beaches in the Caribbean and was a director of the New York Zoological Society. Like all good hunters, he loved animals and spent a lot of time and money protecting them.

It was at home in Ayavalla Plantation that he really enjoyed himself. His happiest hours were spent shooting on his land, which in the winter months was alive with quail, doves, ducks, and wild turkey. The neighboring plantation owners took turns in giving dove shoots and turkey drives. The shooters would ride horses or sometimes sit in the wagons with the shooting dogs.

In the spring and autumn, the fields were made ready for the birds and cattle—seeds were sown and clearings were made.

Ben's most blissful moments were spent driving a bulldozer. He even had an amphibious tractor, bought from Army surplus, which was used to sow algae in the lakes or to drive all the family to the Gulf where it became a pleasure boat from which to swim and fish.

Ben and Klippy celebrated their fiftieth wedding anniversary in June of 1978 with their sons and twelve grandchildren who lived on adjoining plantations.

## The Uninvited Guest

(*Ben's Burglar* as written by Ben himself)

One evening just before Christmas in Westbury House, 1930, Mother and I were in her library when Spike, Michael's pet bull terrier, started to bark. I noticed his head kept turning as he looked through the hall and up the staircase. We decided to investigate, so we went upstairs to the third floor with Spike and opened every room and closet. We came up empty-handed.

On the way down, Klippy went into our dressing room on the second floor to check on presents we were collecting for Christmas, and I went into our bedroom to get a book. Suddenly, Spike rushed under the bed, growling. I yelled at Klippy to bring me my gun—a loaded revolver which I kept next to the bed. She misunderstood me and ran downstairs to find a shotgun and to tell Mother and Father.

There was a man under the bed who threatened to shoot the dog, so I dragged Spike out and got set to kick the intruder on the head as he crawled out. But as he appeared, I thought I recognized Gunnar, our handyman, so I did not kick him. Too late I realized my mistake—he had his hand in his pocket as though he held a weapon and he kept saying, "Stand back, curly head. Keep away." Mother arrived and picked up a heavy, brass doorstop; Klippy came back to say that she couldn't find a gun. And finally, Father, who had read about a crazy man on the loose, came up, unarmed, to see what was going on. A complete stalemate.

*Eleanor Clapp Phipps—"Klippy"*

However, in the course of a long friendly conversation, we all forgot about the pistol. It ended up with Spike sitting on the burglar's lap, while Mother and Klippy went to the pantry to make him some scrambled eggs which they brought up on a silver platter. He told us that he was the son-in-law of a policeman and had worked in our stables some years before, so he knew the place. He had wanted to get some Christmas presents for his children but didn't dare go to his wife's family for money.

I still don't know whether he had a gun in his pocket or not, or why he dove under the bed rather than step out onto the roof the way he had come in. He had used the same route that I usually did when I came home later than I should have, but he climbed up the wrong tree. Mine was an easier way.

Finally we became good friends. Father ordered a taxi for him and gave him his train fare back to New York. We all cordially shook hands, and he told Father that he was the finest gentleman he had ever met. Father offered to help find him a job if he would come to the office the next day, but he never appeared.

*Ben and Klippy on their wedding day, Sandwich, Cape Cod, Massachusetts, 1928*

*Hubert B. Phipps and Fay the Pekinese, 1914*

# HUBERT

Hubert was a maverick. The rest of us were rather solid-citizen types, but Hubert liked to be different. He was born with a lame leg and was delicate throughout his childhood. It was hard on him, being lame in a family of sportsmen, though his disability never stopped him from playing polo or tennis, fox hunting, or enthusiastically chasing the girls. It did, however, rule out his being a top athlete or taking part in the Second World War.

We never spoke of his lameness and neither did he. On looking back, I realize that it would have been better had we not been so protective of him. He always enjoyed a good fight, especially as, when things got too hot, he could count on two or three husky brothers or cousins to come quickly to his rescue. We seldom really fought among ourselves, but we all had explosive tempers, and physical battles without rancor were frequent. Here, Hubert was not at a disadvantage as his hands were like iron.

His scholastic career was a diversified one. After he left St. Bernard's Day School in New York and St. Paul's in Massachusetts, he went to the University of Virginia and then to Oxford. He thoroughly enjoyed both universities and used these picturesque seats of learning as a base for his hunting and racing life as well as for his rather half-hearted academic endeavors.

Because he was a delicate baby, Hubert was Mother's little ewe lamb. We thought it was pronounced "U-Wee" lamb, so he was nicknamed Tiny Wee. Mother worried about him all her life. When writing to her, Hubert often started off by assuring her that he was well and not doing anything foolish. It is also obvious from these letters that he had a great capacity for enjoying life; he had grand times— racing, hunting, and going to parties. In letters from the University of Virginia in Charlottesville, he told her that he hadn't "had time to be lonely. I have hunted eight days out of nine, won the race at Warrenton with Startack and had a fall on Fascenda. I expect to sell some horses in the next two weeks. . . . The Charlottesville races are coming off this Wednesday and next week the National Foxhound Trials are held here. It seems that when I can't go racing or hunting that they both come to me. . . . I won't be home till Monday as I want to go to a dance in Warrenton. I certainly hope it will be a good one as I feel the need of a spree."

*Dita with Hubert,* left, *and Ben, 1905*

Hubert left Charlottesville after a year and went to Oxford for about three years. During the time that he was there, I spent two terms sharing a house with Betty Sharp, a friend from Foxcroft, and her mother. Before I arrived Hubert wrote that he went to call on Betty and see the house. He found two American girls visiting her. He gave them a luncheon party and took them punting on the river. One of the girls insisted on doing the punting herself and fell in the Isis much to everyone's delight.

*Hubert, 1907—as a baby, be was affectionately called "Tiny Wee."*

*Hubert,* left, *with Ben, 1906*

Above: *Hubert, a member of the tribe, with his horse, Rondo,
c. 1918*
Right: *Fishing on the Cascapedia, Quebec, 1915*

Hubert and our cousin Bradley Martin often went to race meets around the countryside. If they won their bets, there would be a party at Bradley's rooms in Christ Church, Christ Church Street, and Betty and I would be invited. We would sit around the fire drinking red wine and playing endless parlor games well into the night.

I don't think Hubert ever passed exams or graduated from Oxford, but after three happy years, he came home and married Carla Gordon, a member of the Chace family.

Just as Ben became a Floridian, Hubert adopted Virginia as his native land. He bought a house in Warrenton and, later on, a large farm in Marshall in the heart of hunting country. He bought and, with the help of his wife, ran the *Fauquire Democrat, Virginia Breeder,* and *Virginia Hog Magazine.* His accent became extremely Southern and his lively wit took on the flavor of his rural neighbors. He liked to picture himself as a wily, astute horse coper. I once overheard a conversation between him and Father.

"All right, Father, I will give you five hundred dollars for the mare provided you can send her over to my stable by Tuesday without fail." "But Hubert," Father responded, "I don't want to sell you the mare. For the last half hour, I have been trying to give her to you."

Hubert's first marriage ended in divorce. A few years later while visiting one of the various English families whose children had been sent to us during the Second World War, he fell in love with one of the younger generation whom he had known as a child at Westbury. He married Phoebe Pleydell Bouverie; of this marriage there were two children.

Though I loved all my brothers equally, Hubert was perhaps the closest to me. Ben was the oldest and Michael the baby, so Hubert and I were the in-betweens. We shared our first hunter and our first car, and we were allies against a kindly but perhaps a bit stuffy world. We had a common love of books and fox hunting, and he was the most amusing of companions.

*Young polo players,* from left, *Ben Phipps, Bobby Young, Hubert Phipps, Harry Cram, and Bradley Martin, c. 1917*

*Helen Margaret ("Peggie") Phipps wearing a favorite dress, embroidered with water lilies, Westbury House, 1912*

# PEGGIE

My own first memory is of a large room with red curtains at the windows and a crackling fire in the fireplace. Outside it was winter, and I could sense the bare branches of the trees. The room was filled with a feeling of cheerfulness and security. Mother said that if I really did remember this scene, it was in the nursery at Dalby Hall in Melton Mowbray in Derbyshire, a house which Father had rented for the fox hunting season and for my expected arrival. I was taken there from the London Nursing Home where I was born on November 17, 1906. I was brought to Westbury when I was about two months old, and I have lived here ever since. Westbury House and I are twins, both having come into existence in the same year. I was lucky that there were already two boys in the nurseries before I appeared. As an only girl in an American family, I was privileged and spoiled by my parents and brothers. But I well remember one summer when we had been sent to a seaside resort with our English cousins. The situation was quite different; besides being bossed around by the male cousins in the house, when we went to church in the village of Bexhill, the older boys walked on one side of the street, and my cousin, Doreen, and I had to stay on the other side with the nurses and babies. The Lords of Creation completely ignored our existence until we got home safely away from the public eye. Then I would revert to my natural place in the pecking order, but Doreen would continue to be subservient. It made a lasting impression on me. Later in life, I learned how deeply ingrained is this male sentiment; however, even though I climbed trees, swam, fished, and took boxing lessons with my brothers, I never wanted to be a boy.

For years we all went to dancing classes to the delight of the little girls and the disgust, feigned or real, of the boys. The mothers of the neighborhood would take turns at having the classes at their houses. Mother also had private lessons at home for Michael and me. Michael did the Irish jig, and I dreamt of becoming a ballet dancer. The dancing teacher was a great help when we had pageants or plays.

When we were ten, nine, and eight, Ben, Hubert, and I went to a branch of St. Bernard's School which had two small houses in Westbury village. The girls' division had eight girls and one boy. I don't know

*Dita with Peggie, 1906*

why poor Freddy Nicholas was put in with the girls, but he was useful because he ate up all that was left in our lunchboxes, and we were not scolded for leaving some of our sandwiches.

Here I made my first friend who was not a member of the family. Barbara Sands was a large, handsome girl; she lived with her guardian, Ogden Mills, in Woodbury just down the Jericho Turnpike. She had a very severe English governess who, luckily for us, was a great friend of my governess, so there was a lot of visiting between houses. Barbara knew all the facts of life—or at least thought she did. Some-

*Peggie at Battle Abbey, 1906*

how she· had acquired an almost lifesize skeleton which she kept under her bed. It wasn't really a skeleton but a cardboard model of the human body with the organs in layers between the bones. As soon as our governesses were safely downstairs gossiping over their tea, we would rush up to her room and pull out the body from under her bed and study it with guilty interest.

When the boys and I were sent to school in New York, I lost sight of Barbara. I heard later that she had eloped with a Naval officer at the age of eighteen. She is one of my few intimate friends who did not last me a lifetime.

When I was eleven, I went to school at Miss Chapin's, then on Fifty-seventh Street in New York. This was a strict and fashionable school. I don't remember what I learned there, but I'm sure it gave me a good grounding for future education. Still, I never can see why one wastes time learning Latin and mathematics when there are such interesting subjects as history, literature, and living languages.

It was fortunate that although my division was the lowest and the dumbest one in the class, in it

were all the nicest and most attractive girls. On several occasions, Mother complained to the headmistress that I was too bright to be in the dumb division. Miss Chapin answered dryly that "it was hard to evaluate Margaret's mental capacity" as I spent most of the winter in Palm Beach.

A few weeks after my second year at school, a new girl arrived in class. She was tall and thin with spindly legs and masses of soft brown hair. Everyone loved her, and she was besieged with requests—"Sit beside me, I've saved a chair for you." Soon it was accepted automatically that she and I sat beside each other. There must have been some family attraction that Ben and I shared because this girl was Eleanor Klapp and not only did Klippy and I become inseparable friends, but she eventually married my brother.

Klippy was a constant visitor at Westbury and even went abroad with us to Scotland and Spain. In turn, I would stay with her in Sandwich on Cape Cod. Her family had a lovely old house on the outskirts of the village, overlooking a large pond. Mr. and Mrs. Klapp were Quakers, and I first heard the spoken "thee" and "thou" when Klippy's mother said, "Nellie dear, when is thee going to get thy teeth fixed?" These visits were a new and delightful experience for me. We had complete freedom to go into the village, take long walks in the country, and even to go alone to the movies where an energetic pianist thumped out the accompaniment to the films.

When I was sixteen and Malcolm Chace's daughter Eliot was seventeen, the Phipps and the Chace families decided they would send their daughters to Paris to a finishing school. As a result, Eliot and I went to Mademoiselle Lacareres in Neuilly. It really was not a top school. There were about fifteen of us from all different countries, and none of us was very serious about learning French. If I had only known that I was eventually going to marry a Frenchman! Mother had insisted that I have a governess to board nearby in case I was ill or something. As it turned out, I was quite dangerously ill for about ten days, and she was useful for a while. In a rush of sentiment and anxiety at leaving his only daughter in a strange country so far from home, Father had told the French doctor to give me two smallpox vaccinations instead of one. They both took beautifully, and I was confined to my bed with a raging fever. When I was recovering, Mademoiselle sent me up some calves brain in jelly. It was a delicate attention but revolting. The jelly was so firm that Eliot and I played ball with it for a few minutes and then tossed it out the window. We were not fond of Mademoiselle. She toadied to the richer girls, and we were only allowed to have one bath a week. Nonetheless, there were nice things about the school too. The main house was set in an old-fashioned garden, and there were small studios in the shrubbery where I spent many hours practicing the piano. Every Tuesday, we would visit the Louvre accompanied by a professor. After two hours of admiring all "Les Merveilles," we went to Rumplemeyers for tea, where we gorged ourselves on ices, éclairs, and meringue nests filled with purée of chestnuts and crème chantilly.

After a year in France, I went to Foxcroft, in Middleburg, Virginia. Having heard about the school from all sides, I was longing to go there; however, I hadn't enrolled for the coming year, and there were no extra places. Father, Mother, and I went down to Middleburg to plead my case. We met the famous headmistress of Foxcroft, Miss Charlotte Noland. She was a most charming, energetic, and, I thought, rather childish person. We were taken to see her best friend who owned a stable next door. Father bought a nice little hunter for me, and I was accepted at school. There I spent two happy years. Mondays were free days, and if you owned or rented a horse, you were allowed to go out with the Middleburg hunt which was great fun. In the spring, we would be taken on long picnic rides through the lovely countryside. The woods were filled with white dogwood and pale magenta Judas trees; the creeks were swollen with winter rain, and always there were the Blue Ridge Mountains in the distance.

From left, *Hubert, Ben, and Peggie, at Fairlawn, Newport, 1907*

*Dita with her children at Southampton, Long Island, 1909:* from left, *Peggie, Hubert, and Ben*

Here, for the first time, I was really on my own. It had been suggested that I would find it hard, as a spoiled and only daughter, to be thrown in amongst over one hundred competitive girls; also, it was hinted that it might take me down a peg or two. It proved to be just the opposite. After one week of miserable homesickness, I quickly found a good place for myself in the school. I always was fond of studying, and I made friends easily, so my self-confidence went up several pegs. The encouragements and compliments of one's parents, though kindly meant, are usually taken with a large grain of salt. Any normal child is skeptical of family admiration. It is only when you do something on your own that you find out where you stand in life. At the end of two years, I graduated head of my class.

After completing school, along with all the other girls of my age, I became a debutante. The family had the red drawing room at Westbury enlarged into a ballroom for my coming out party, but since it was not ready by the time I reached almost eighteen, I had the party at Sherries, the fashionable hotel of that time.

The debutante parties of those days were very glamorous and rather frightening. You could easily spot a "belle" by the long stag line following her, eager to cut in for a minute or so before another beau touched him on the shoulder to claim his

*High tea, 1909:* from left, *Hubert, Ben, and Peggie*

142

*Hubert and Peggie with Nanny and an entertaining friend*

partner. The popular girls had too many partners, and the stags were afraid to cut in on the girls who were shy or perhaps didn't know many boys, because they might get stuck and have to spend an embarrassing, long time with each other. This was a cruel distribution of pleasure. I was lucky in that I always had a brother or a cousin in the stag lines who would rescue me if I gave them a signal of distress.

As the years went by, I discovered that the lives of the so-called belles and their opposites, the "pills," turned out much alike, their success or failure depending on luck and character. Klippy and I were neither belles nor pills, but we were shy with boys and apprehensive about our social lives. One night I dreamed a dream that was so vivid I can remember every detail to this day. There was a dance at Westbury and being left for a moment without a partner, I wandered into the billiard room. Here was a safe haven for me. The room was empty, so I crawled under the billiard table which, in my dream, was completely covered with a long green baize cloth. Somebody else was there before me and moved in the darkness. It was Klippy! Dear Klippy, she became a well-known beauty and a charming hostess to all Ben's hunting, shooting, and political friends.

When the ballroom was finally finished, we had many other parties there. We danced and we danced. We played tennis on the south lawn. We swam in the pool or at Piping Rock. We rode and played golf. Very

*Peggie, one of the "Mohicans" on the lake at Westbury House, c. 1913*

Fourth of July celebration, Westbury House, 1916. The children are dressed as the allied nations of World War I and symbols of peace and liberty: standing from left, *Lillias Kent (representing France), Hubert Phipps (U.S. Army), Peggie Phipps (Great Britain), Hope Iselin, (The United States), Hope Livermore (Liberty), Francesca Livermore (Peace), Ben Phipps (Uncle Sam), Barbara Sands (Russia), Alice de Forest (Italy), Ogden Phipps (U.S. Army) and Barbara Phipps (Belgium);* seated, left, *Michael Phipps (U.S. Navy) and,* right, *Pat Livermore (U.S. Navy).*

*Spectating at Mineola, Long Island, 1911:* from left, *Peggie, Mrs. H. C. (Gladys Mills) Phipps holding her son Ogden;* foreground, *Hal Phipps*

few of the boys and none of the girls worked during the holidays. There seemed to be an endless round of amusements. We fell in and out of love two or three times a year. (In those days, boys did not proposition you; they solemnly proposed marriage.)

In June the air was filled with the scent of honeysuckle and new-mown hay. The cicadas and the tree toads strummed their songs throughout the warm summer nights. By July the first, bursts of firecrackers could be heard from the village where the patriotic Italians and Poles could not wait for Independence Day. All the excitement of the summer season culminated in a Fourth of July dance and fireworks at the Piping Rock Club.

In the years before we moved to the Piping Rock Club for our Fourth of July celebration, we had our own fireworks at home. Father was master of ceremonies. We all gathered around him on the south lawn while he set off the charges—starting with the smaller ones and ending with a burst of Katherine wheels. Once, in an absent-minded moment, he stood by the box of fireworks with a lighted sparkler in his hand. All of a sudden, a spark ignited a cracker, and there was the most glorious display of fireworks shooting in all directions. It was all over in a few minutes. Some of us ran, and others just stood there

*Peggie in the Irish lace dress that tickled, Westbury House, 1909*

*Peggie and Ben, in their costumes for* Midsummer Night's Dream, *1914 -*

*A private performance of* Midsummer Night's Dream *in Palm Beach, 1914:* from left, *Lillias Kent as Pea Blossom, Barbara Phipps as Cobwell, Michael Phipps as Mustard Seed, Ben as Bottom, and Peggie as Queen Titania*

transfixed between terror and amusement. Another Fourth of July, Mother had the patriotic idea of dressing us up as heroes and emblems of the first Independence Day.

After Ben and Klippy got married in 1928, I felt rather at a loss, so I persuaded the family to let me go to Oxford to spend the winter terms there with my Foxcroft friend, Betty Sharp, and her mother. This was an unqualified success. Mrs. Sharp had rented Christ Church House from a don who was taking his sabbatical year abroad. It was on the Banbury Road across the Magdalene Bridge by the playing fields and the River Isis. We could hear the bells of Magdalene and Christ Church tolling the hours just as they had done in the time of Henry VIII and Elizabeth I. They filled the air with that immemorial sound of peace and beauty, as they had chimed before to countless young men eager for life and learning, as they had tolled for the dead, and had rung out in wild joy for victories and celebrations. In our time, they were bells that gently marked the time of day and gave a promise of centuries to come.

We went to our tutors in sweaters and skirts and the inevitable raincoat. In fact, we paid so little attention to our clothes that when Billy Astor, the American Lady Astor's son, invited me to a house party at Hever Castle for the Christmas holidays I declined, partly out of shyness but also because I had absolutely nothing to wear. I'm sorry now because George Bernard Shaw was a member of the party, and it would have given me a fascinating memory.

Unfortunately, I always let my shyness get the better of me, and it wasn't until I was running Westbury Gardens and absolutely had to meet people and even make speeches that I conquered this bugbear. With the exception of the Guest family and maybe Michael, all the Phippses and Martins were burdened with an excessive shyness. It was as though our Fairy Godmother had endowed us with so many good things—health, wealth, and a fair amount of looks and intelligence—all to be overshadowed by the painful gift of shyness from the Wicked Witch.

Coming back after my winter in Oxford, I wanted to do something more than just live at home. I never liked the people in Palm Beach, and our apartment at One Sutton Place was just too grand for my way of life. So Mother rented a small apartment for me and loaned me one of her maids. I moved in with Anne Colby, a very sweet and extremely pretty friend of mine from Foxcroft. We decided to get a job in a bookshop. Since we went out quite a lot at night and both needed eight hours of sleep, we tried for one job that we could divide between us. In that way, each of us could sleep late every second morning. Nobody seemed to want us under these circumstances. Then, one day, Anne found a small shop in the seventies, run by a Russian who said that he would accept us. I proudly told my family about our job. Father asked Mr. Layman, the head of Bessemer, the Phipps office, to look into the situation. It turned out that though the front room of the shop was most

suitable, pornographic books were sold in the back room—so that was out. Mr. Layman, who was not only the head of the office, but also a kind friend, said he knew of a clever young woman who had been running the library on a ship and could most likely help us with a bookshop. And so we met Ilah Nichoff—liked her on first sight—and with her help, opened the Wakefield Bookshop on Madison Avenue and 53rd Street. Ilah ran it with two of my more intellectual friends from Foxcroft and me.

Anne Colby soon left to get married to Bill Vanderbilt, but she did her best to be useful before the shop opened. On the first day, she and Bill arrived with blue smocks they had bought for all the sales ladies, and they spent the morning putting up the bookshelves. Unfortunately, they placed the shelves too close together for the size of the average book,

From left, *Barbara, Michael, Ogden, and Peggie Phipps, Raymond Guest, Lillias Kent, Winston Guest, and Ben and Hubert Phipps*

*Dancing on the lawn, Westbury House, 1914*

*Dancers at rest:* from left, *Peggie, Lillias Kent, Alice de Forest, Hope Livermore, Hope Iselin, and Barbara Sands*

*Peggie,* à point, *Westbury House, 1916*

and the work had to be done over. The smocks, however, were very becoming!

Our work at the shop was both interesting and fun. Naturally, we read a lot of books, and we were all enchanted with Irish literature. Also, we met with a wide variety of people and predicaments. There was one little old lady who spent the whole morning looking for books only to decide, "I think perhaps my husband would rather have a tie." When she was gone, we found there were some books missing. There was another embarrassing moment when Bibles were ordered for all the Mellon grandchildren—they arrived printed *Mellen* according to my spelling.

The Wakefield Bookshop ran for twenty-eight years before it was bought by Joan Whitney and joined with Young Books.

On October 2, 1930, I married Gordon Douglas. When we came home from our honeymoon, the family gave us a house in the garden at Westbury. It was and is a charming, late nineteenth-century farmhouse painted white with green shutters; its countrylike name was Orchard Hill. We were supposed to stay there only until my baby was born. Dita II arrived on the Fourth of July of that year, but we never moved out of the house. Four years later, Gordon III was born.

During the Second World War, Gordon was a lieutenant in the naval station. I became a nurse's aide and worked in the hospitals wherever he was stationed. We also adopted two English children for the duration and were rewarded for this act of kindness by acquiring their marvelous Scottish governess who brought up all four children and stayed with us

*The dancer and the doll, Westbury House, 1914; the piano was carried from the ballroom for outdoor dance classes.*

*Ballerina, Westbury House, 1914*

*Peggie Phipps on the staircase at Westbury House, just before her wedding to James Gordon Douglas II, July 1929*

for eleven years. After the war, Gordon and I obtained an amicable divorce.

When I was living in New York City, a friend and I took a course in psychology at Columbia University. The students were of all ages though, of course, we were among the oldest ones. I was quite prepared to be embarrassed by some of the subjects discussed by modern young people on a modern subject, so I was not bothered. One day I was late for class and the professor turned to me and explained, "We are speaking about spirits." I thought, how nice. Here is a subject that interests me and I know something about. So I made a few innocent remarks treating spirits and ghosts as mysterious but natural phenomena of our world. The professor was shocked—really shocked—as well as seriously annoyed. He acted as though I had insulted his intelligence, and he never again asked me to speak in class. Why would a teacher of psychology be afraid of ghosts? Even if he didn't believe in them and discounted all the eyewitness stories, still he would have to admit that they are creatures of that marvelous and little-known object, the human mind.

Fortunetellers are usually associated with the spirit world, I suppose because they see things that others cannot. When we were young and foolish, some of my friends had their futures truly predicted, but I was never told anything that made sense until I was about forty years of age. One evening I was dining with Ben and Klippy at a nightclub when a palmist came up to our table and asked to read our palms. She told me that I was going to be married for the second time very happily and that my husband's name would be Stephen. I didn't know any Stephen, so I thought no more about it. A year or two later, on June 16, 1951, I married Etienne Boegner, a French Protestant and son of the illustrious Pastor Marc Boegner, head of the Huguenot Church and member of the French Academy. One day Etienne said to me, "This is my saint's day. You can give me a present if you want." I answered, "But it isn't your birthday, what do you mean?" He looked surprised, then said, "Didn't you know that my name in English is Stephen? This is St. Stephen's Day."

We continued to live in Orchard Hill with his three children and my two—so life at Westbury followed its accustomed course. Only now, it was the turn for grandchildren to play in the gardens, to have tea with Grandma on the West Porch, and, later, for the granddaughters to dance in the ballroom at their coming-out parties.

*Peggie with her son Gordon, 1938*

*Gordon Douglas II, a lieutenant in the U.S. Navy, with his son also in "uniform," 1942*

*Three generations of Douglases, Westbury House, c. 1940*

Left: *Peggie, Mrs. Etienne Boegner, 1951*
Below: *Peggie, her granddaughter DeeDee Amory, and Etienne Boegner in the Walled Garden at Westbury House*

*The receiving line, Westbury House ballroom, at Dita Douglas' coming out party, 1948. Greeting the guests are three generations of Phippses: from left, Gordon Douglas, Dita Douglas, Peggie Phipps Douglas, and Dita Phipps.*

158

*Michael G. Phipps, 1914*

# MICHAEL

Michael was the jewel of the family, a card, and a pickle. He had all the talents, looks, and charm, combined with a very sweet nature. Everyone loved him. From my point of view, thank heavens he wasn't a girl; still, I envied his beautiful grey eyes with their long black lashes. When he was a child, he played the piano well and was good at drawing, so good, in fact, that at an early age he managed to sell sketches of nudes to his classmates for five cents each. At college, he became quite serious about his painting, and he might have become an artist, but his life did not follow that path.

I remember one day during the time when we were at Miss Chapin's school, Klippy and another friend, Sophie Gay, and I decided to cook our lunch in the open fireplace at the thatch cottage. None of us really knew how to cook since girls didn't in those days. At any rate, we had a roasting chicken on top of the grill, and it seemed to be doing pretty well; then, all of a sudden, it was gone. Michael had climbed onto the roof and, with a hook attached to a stick, had speared the chicken by way of the chimney and run away with it. A cheeky boy and three years younger, he was a gadfly to me and my friends—teasing and playing jokes on us. When he stole my diary, he found it filled with complaints about him. I think, perhaps, he was hurt. He shouldn't have been, for we all unquestioningly loved each other; and any criticism would have been purely a form of temporary irritation.

It is funny, but I have noticed that people with plenty of money really enjoy their pet economies. Father and the boys economized on their clothes. They had some nice clothes, but they absolutely never seemed to have anything new. I can still see Father's black shoes with elastic sides which cost him $4.50. He was very proud of them, but to Mother and me, they made him pathetic. In the same vein, when Michael was at St. Paul's, I went to school to take him out for lunch and I remember how happy he and his friend Drayton Cochran were because they had discovered that by inking-in places on their legs the holes in their Sunday stockings didn't show. I also recall that the two boys had arranged for a picnic in a canoe but somehow the canoe tipped over and we never did have our lunch.

*Dita and her youngest child, Michael, 1912*

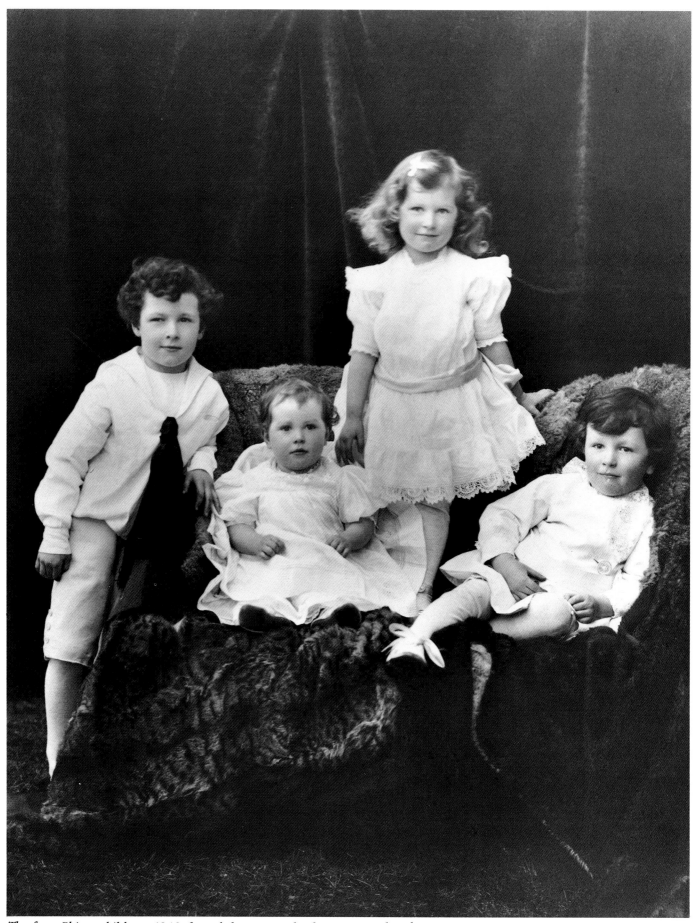

*The four Phipps children, 1912:* from left, *Ben, Michael, Peggie, and Hubert*

*Michael, Palm Beach, 1915*

Michael started practicing polo when he was eight or nine years old under the guidance of Father and Mrs. Thomas Hitchcock. This beginners group sometimes included two or three girls. The games were usually played on our practice field, and Helen Hitchcock, Diana Guest, and I usually joined in. Later, when Michael was at New Haven, he became a member of the Yale polo team. He went on from there to play number one for the American International Team. His position as a ten-goal player took up much of his time, and he often traveled to England, India, and South America for international matches. It was at a polo party in Calcutta that he met Molly Lane, soon to be his beautiful English wife. A few months later, he proposed to her by long distance from Westbury to Cairo where she had gone for the races.

When first married, Ben and Michael, like me, lived in white wooden houses on the family's grounds. Hubert was already in Virginia. Ben and Klippy then moved south to Tallahassee, Michael and Molly divided their time between Westbury and Palm Beach, and I stayed in Westbury and enlarged our house. Like all of us, Michael had a real love of the country and all that goes with it—space and trees and animals—so when he and Molly started to spend much of their time in Palm Beach and built a house there, Michael bought a cattle ranch in Stuart, Florida, an hour from Palm Beach by helicopter.

*Master of the Irish jig, Westbury, 1916*

*Michael on his pony, Indian, with his uncle, Hal Phipps, c. 1918*

My three brothers were cattlemen. Ben had Charolais, Hubert a herd of Black Angus, and Michael Santa Gertrudis. I never could figure out whether they made money on their cattle ventures, but anyhow it kept them happy, and, in the long run, it proved to be worthwhile, for each bought great tracts of land in Florida and Virginia before the prices went soaring.

Michael spent most of the war in England with the Air Force Intelligence of the 8th Bomber Group and in Africa with the 12th Bomber Squadron. He went as an observer on several raids. He was a rather exceptionally brave person, but I have a letter in which he wrote, "Don't let Gordon be disappointed at not seeing active service. My experience here is that one is either bored or scared to death." Sometimes though he must have enjoyed himself when stationed in London, as he stayed at the house of Mother's sister, our Aunt Gladys Benskin. Forty Belgrave Square became more or less a club for his many American friends and was known as Hotel Belgravia.

After the war, Michael again took up his polo, painting, and ranching. His life was one of unparalleled success and happiness until he was about sixty years of age. Then, his wife Molly died, followed a few years later by Nonie, their elder daughter; and Michael himself did not survive them for very long. He left one daughter, Susie Cochran, and her three children, Jay, Angela, and Cecelia.

*Michael hunting with Spike, c. 1925*

164

*Michael, ten-goal polo player*

*At the start of a polo pony race, Westbury, 1927*

*Dita and Michael, c. 1927*

*The winning team, National Open Polo Championship 1937:* from left, *Michael Phipps, C. Smith, Stewart Iglehart, and C. V. Whitney*

*The wedding party—Michael, Molly Lane Phipps, and Spike—Casa Bendita, Palm Beach, 1936*

*Harry and Annie Phipps and their youngest child Howard, c. 1912*

# GRANDPA & GRANDMA

My memories of Grandpa Phipps are very sparse. By the time I knew him, he had already been ill for several years and his mind was wandering. Today, there are over a hundred of his descendants who are enjoying the fortune that he worked so hard and so brilliantly to create for his family. Yet, none of us except his sons and daughters ever really knew him or even about him. He always shunned fame and publicity.

To me, he was just a dear, vague little old man. When we were taken to Bonnie Blink, his Great Neck home, to visit him and Grandma, he was usually propped up in bed or resting on a chaise longue on the porch. He could recite poetry by the hour, and, as he wasn't always sure where he was, I felt that he was actually seeing the beauties of the poems that he was quoting. One day when we were there, he was reciting Byron and thought he was in Venice.

He came to Westbury a few times when we were small. We thought him funny because he couldn't understand that we were all his grandchildren. He would point to one of us and say, "Whose little boy or girl are you?" The only time he came for lunch, Hubert's Sealyham terrier was under the table and bit him on the leg—which was shocking, but funny too.

I feel sad that such a good and fascinating character should be so little known to all of us. I think it admirable that Grandpa, having worked so hard to earn his money, was so generous in giving it away to charities. Following his example, his children gave to the Girl Scouts and to hospitals, and donated parks to Florida and New Jersey, while his grandchildren have supported the New York Zoological Society and the American Museum of Natural History, and have preserved Old Westbury Gardens for the public. In each case, a family member has been a hard-working president of the above organizations.

My Grandma Phipps was rather tall and thin and held herself very straight. To me she seemed the perfect example of an American lady of the nineteenth century, with the religious faith, strict morality, and good sense and proper manners that that implies. This was partly because she really was

From left, *Malcolm Chace, Annie, Harry, and Jay,* c. 1910

a kindly person and also because she was a Christian Scientist and practiced the Christian Science smile. When she was a young girl, the doctors told her that she was going blind and that there was nothing to do about it. She became a follower of Mary Baker Eddy and was completely cured. In fact, her eyesight was so good that even as an old lady she seldom had to wear glasses.

When I first read the letters Grandma wrote as a young woman, my portrait of her as a grandmother and the typical American grande dame had already been well established in my mind. How different she had been as a young married woman, having to find her way in a new life. Yet throughout the years, her kindness and a certain form of American puritanism remained unchanged.

Grandma came from a poor but well-educated family. She was eleven years younger than Grandpa, and she must have been the most unselfish and devoted wife. Years before I remember her, she had adapted herself to her husband's rise in fortune and position. Mrs. Fred Allen, our family friend, told me, "Mr. and Mrs. Phipps would have large house parties in the castles that they rented in England and Scotland. As well as old friends, Mrs. Phipps would invite people whom she thought interesting because they had

*Annie and her son Jay, c. 1927*

written a book or were sponsoring a good cause. Every evening she would preside at dinner, beautifully dressed by Worth, and enjoy her role as a hostess until 9:30 P.M.; then Mr. Phipps would appear from the library and say, 'It's bedtime, Mother.' She would immediately bid her guests goodnight and join him." In later years when Grandpa was ill, she looked after him with the most devoted care.

When I first knew my grandparents, they lived in a marble house on Fifth Avenue at Eighty-seventh Street, set back from the street by a lawn and a driveway. After several years, they sold this house and built a Georgian house on Long Island close to Westbury where their five children lived. They also had a small house in West Palm Beach that had originally been bought by Grandma for a member of her family.

From the long list of public charities and many grateful private letters that I found, it is obvious that Grandma took great pleasure in sharing her good fortune with others.

Like many of the women in our family, Grandma was a matriarch. Her five children adored her and obeyed her unquestioningly right up to the end. When the inheritance tax was becoming a law, she waited until the very last moment before signing over her husband's fortune to her children. Naturally, the family and the Bessemer office were in a turmoil.

I remember one winter in Palm Beach, long after we were all grown up, Father had a bad bout of the flu. As he was recovering, the doctor said that he must get up and move around a bit, but Father refused; neither Mother nor Michael could get him to budge. Finally, in desperation, Mother telephoned Grandma. She immediately came over from West Palm Beach to Casa Bendita, our house in Palm Beach, and sent up word that Mrs. Phipps, Sr., was waiting in the loggia for Mr. Phipps. Father was down in no time flat. It turned out that all this excitement was unnecessary, as Father later admitted that he had been in the habit of stealing downstairs to raid the pantry icebox every night while the nurse was off duty.

The summer that the Prince of Wales was here, he played several matches on our polo fields. He sent word to Father that he would like to come to tea. For this occasion, we were all dressed in our best. and Grandma was invited. She was delighted to meet the prince, but she didn't think it proper that an elderly American lady should stand up for any young man whoever he was. Father was rather nervous. However, as the prince came into the drawing room he quickly walked over to where Grandma was sitting, and taking her hand, he said, "Mrs. Phipps, your son has been so kind. I have enjoyed playing on his polo field."

*Annie with three of her great-grandchildren, at Bonnie Blink, c. 1930*

When Grandma moved to Long Island, she became a friend of Robert Moses and would drive around the countryside with him looking for possible sites for parks or parkways. This was a rather peculiar companionship because the Phipps family must have been among those who successfully opposed Mr. Moses' plan to put the Northern State Parkway through the middle of Old Westbury. Thwarted on the plan for his road, he wrote an article about the mushroom millionaires of Old Westbury who aped the English aristocracy with their large houses, beautifully kept gardens, polo fields, and fox hunting. This was hardly fair for up to that time, the early 1900s, most of the Long Island families were of British descent, and the climate and the countryside lent themselves naturally to the English way of life.

Now the Long Island Expressway does run through Old Westbury, and it hasn't done much harm. In fact, it would be impossible for Long Islanders to get to New York at all if we didn't have it and the other parkways designed by Mr. Moses. It was his vision that preserved the miles and miles of Jones Beach that are now enjoyed by millions of people from the city and the island.

Mr. Moses and his assistants were also of the greatest help to us when we opened the gardens to visitors. He was sensitive to the feel of the place and warned us not to turn it over to the state or county but to give it to the public and keep the running of it in the family. He graciously accepted our invitation to be the speaker at the opening ceremonies.

After Grandpa's death, Grandma moved over to live with her daughter, Aunt Helen Martin, at Knole, Westbury, where she peacefully spent her last years, confident that she would join her beloved husband.

*Michael Paul Grace—"Grandpoods"—c. 1885*

# GRANDPOODS & GRANDMOODS

In the library at Westbury there is a large, white vellum tome, embossed in gold, privately printed in London in 1911. The title reads, *The Family of Grace: Pedigrees and Memoirs,* collected and edited by the Reverend Joseph Wilhem, D.D. The author traced the Grace family from the eleventh century when Le Gras, Le Graso, or Grassus came to England with William the Conqueror. The line continues down through thirty generations to my great-grandfather, James Grace, who married Ellen Russell and had seven children. Their seventh son, born in 1842 in Ireland, was Michael Paul, my grandfather.

During the famine that gripped Ireland in the mid-nineteenth century, my great-grandfather James Grace provided work for the people on his Ballylinan estate and for his neighbors, often paying them their wages before they had been earned. Later, when James had settled in Peru, he brought over two hundred Irish emigrants to work on sugar plantations.

William Russell Grace, my grandfather's eldest brother, also settled in Peru and joined the firm of John Bryce, General Merchandise and Shipping; it later became Grace Brothers and Company, when my grandfather, Michael Paul, joined the firm after attending college in Lima.

It was during this time that my grandfather made the acquaintance of the Earl of Donoughmore, who was one of the original partners of Bryce and Company. Their friendship lasted through the years, and eventually Elena Grace, my aunt, married Viscount Suirdale, the son and heir of Lord Donoughmore.

The Grace firm rapidly grew to importance and became the leading American house on the west coast of South America. During the American Civil War, Mr. Grace placed the resources of his shipping line at the disposal of the vessels of the American Navy when all others refused credit to the United States. In 1864, because of ill health, W. R. Grace went to live in the United States. He was made head of the firm of W. R. Grace in New York and later became mayor of New York City. He bought a house, Gracefield, in Great Neck, and today, many of his descendants are still living on Long Island.

When, in turn, Michael P. Grace left Peru, he joined his brother again, this time in New York. Then, after three years, he took his wife—Margarita (Ma-

*Margarita Mason Grace—"Grandmoods"—Lima, Peru, 1879*

From left, *Ben and Peggie Phipps, Lucy and Evelyn ("Pickles") Webster, and Hubert Phipps at Battle Abbey, 1906*

*Grandpoods and the peacock, Battle Abbey, England, c. 1904*

son)—and four daughters—Elisa, Elena, Margarita (my mother), and Gladys—to live permanently in London, where he became head of the British branch of Grace Brothers.

The Grace family had many philanthropic interests, but the Grace Institute, founded by the brothers William and Michael, was one of the most widely used. The object was to provide protection and assistance to young women and to furnish instruction in domestic arts and sciences, for these were the trades and occupations in which women were then employed.

Grandpoods, as we called Mother's father, was small and round, with pink cheeks, bright blue eyes, and a sparkling look. Without the slightest effort on his part he charmed everyone and made them feel that they were of the utmost importance. He lavished his affections on his four daughters and nine grandchildren. Each one of us secretly felt that he or she was his favorite.

When we were children, he spent half the year with us or we with him. He would stay at Westbury for a few weeks in the autumn, and then we would

*Grandpoods and Dita at Battle Abbey, c. 1904*

spend the winter with him in one of the Breakers' cottages in Palm Beach. In the spring, he would stop by on his way to England, and we joined him and the rest of the Michael Grace family for August and September. So for me, he was the inmost part of the family along with Mother, Father, my brothers, and my dog. I found one of his old calling cards, engraved with his name and two addresses: "Incas," Palm Beach, and Westbury House, Westbury, Long Island. So, for him also, his American family was his second home.

Though Grandpoods went to Florida for the winter and took a shooting moor in Scotland each summer, mostly for the sake of his sons-in-law, the place he really loved was Battle Abbey in Kent. There he lived like a country squire surrounded by his family, cousins, and friends, and it was from there that he gave in marriage his two youngest daughters— my mother and Aunt Glad.

I think 40 Belgrave Square in London must have been home to Grandmoods, and Battle Abbey to Grandpoods. The attractive village of Battle on Kent consists of a broad main street leading up to the Abbey gates. The gates are flanked by two large towers with an archway between them and a high stone wall on either side. One could walk along to the top of the wall, getting a bird's-eye view of the village and the churchyard. Some steps led down to the circular rose garden and to a terraced garden sloping to the woods and farmland.

Aunt Glad, living there until she was married, found Battle a dull place, a countrified society, a rather poor hunt, and not much to do except go for long walks. My brothers and I found it enchanting. I can still remember the wonderful damp smell of the laurels and rhododendron bushes where we used to hide. I have always loved those shiny, dark-leaved plants and trees which we treasure in America, but are so common in England.

There were a lot of exciting things to do and see. If we weren't accompanying Nanny pushing Michael's pram through the lanes, we were allowed to play in the gardens. They weren't ordinary gardens—somewhere in the shrubbery there was the opening to a tunnel that led from the Abbey to Hastings-on-the-Sea, six miles away. A monk in peril could escape to the seashore by this tunnel and set sail for France. Along with terraces, there were places made of a different stone from the rest of the walls. This is where the monks or nuns who disobeyed were walled up and left to die.

There were several phantoms on the place. A large white swan sometimes visited one of the spare rooms, and on moonlit nights the ghosts of the monks murdered by Cromwell were seen slowly walking up and down the yew walk that led to the rose garden.

Grandpoods—"Mr. South America"—as depicted by the cartoonist "Spy" for Punch

We were in the habit of carrying salt in our pockets to ward off any spirit. If one threw salt and made the sign of the cross, any evil spirit would have to vanish! (The rose gardens and the ghost walk have been duplicated in the Old Westbury Gardens.)

We also enjoyed more modern amusements. Every Wednesday we could trail after the tourists who came to see the ruins of the original Abbey, which was the chief attraction for sightseers. The roof was gone, but the walls outlined the plan of the long refectory, the cloisters, and the cells. Purple-toad ivy grew between the stones, and the close-cut grass dotted with tiny daisies made an emerald carpet. Nearby stood a small but elaborate stone and blue-enamel monument that marked the spot where King Harold fell in 1066, pierced through the heart by a Norman arrow. For two shillings, tourists were allowed into the great hall of the Abbey, an enormous two-storied baronial hall complete with banners,

*The drawing room, Battle Abbey, c. 1906*

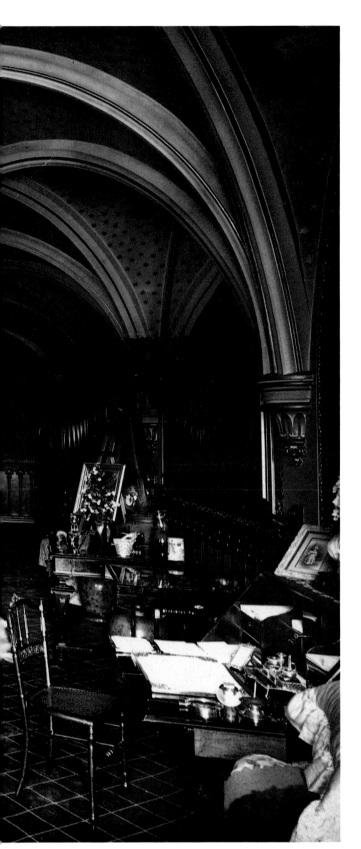

*The gates of Battle Abbey, Aunt Glad at the wheel, c. 1906*

*The great hall, Battle Abbey, c. 1906*

*The Grace grandchildren:* standing, from left, *Ben Phipps, Ordy Suirdale, and Michael Beaumont;* seated, clockwise from lower right, *Peggie, Michael, and Hubert Phipps, David and Doreen Hely-Hutchinson*

knights' armor, and a priest-hole hidden in the upper gallery. They also enjoyed peering in the windows of the drawing room to see the vaulted blue ceiling painted with silver stars and to watch Grandmoods and her friends having tea.

The Websters, who owned Battle Abbey and rented it to Grandpoods on a seven-year basis for twenty-one years, were friends and neighbors. One of the girls, called Pickles, was so pretty that even at that early age we all were under her spell. For some unknown reason, an old gypsy woman had cursed the Webster family by the sword, water, and fire. All of these curses were carried out, and only one of the children, Pickles, survived.

After the First World War when the lease for Battle Abbey had ended, Grandpoods was visiting Aunt Glad in Frant. He said that he would like to see his old home again before he died. She collected all her gasoline rations, and they drove the twenty miles to Battle. Before visiting the Abbey, which had been turned into a school, Grandpoods went into one of the small shops on the village street. Someone must have recognized him because when he came out a few minutes later, the whole village had gathered around to shake his hand and wish him well—no greater tribute could have been paid to royalty.

During the Second World War, the Abbey was turned into a hospital for the soldiers. The patients were delighted by signs beneath the bells in the dormitories, saying "Ring twice for a mistress." In 1976, it was bought by the National Trust, and although the school continues to function, the Abbey grounds are open to visitors.

Grandpoods is buried in the churchyard in Battle Abbey just across from the rose garden wall. On his simple tombstone is engraved this epitaph:

> Cordial Old Man
> What youth was in thy years
> What wisdom in thy levity
> What kindness in every utterance
>     of that pure soul

Few of the spirits of the glorified
I'd spring to earlier at the gates
of heaven

and beneath a tombstone beside him lies his wife,
Margarita Manson Grace.

*Dita, Peggie, and Grandpoods, Westbury House, c. 1918*

B y the time I knew my English grandparents,
their life in Ireland, South America, and New
York was far behind them. For many years, Grandmoods had been established in one of those handsome cream-colored houses in Belgrave Square.
Seeing her again in memory, Grandmoods looked
just the way a London grandmother should—her oval
face with its great violet eyes and hawklike little nose,
her abundant white hair swept up from her forehead
and surrounded by a lovely hat of gauze and ostrich
plumes. Her clothes were silky, in all shades of grey,
and large drop earrings matched the many strings of
pearl necklaces around her neck. From way back
in her South American past she spoke with a slight
and most attractive accent.

All the houses on the square belonged to the
Duke of Sutherland and could not be sold. Forty
Belgrave Square, therefore, was on a seventy-year
lease which ended when my aunt let it run out in
the early 1960s.

*Grandpoods, 1912*

Even now Belgrave Square is still beautiful. The
five-story houses, which are all of the same design
except for a slightly more elaborate architecture on
the corners, frame the four sides of a large garden
to which the owners have keys. I can remember
playing on the shady paths and well-kept lawns. When
Mother was young, every house had flower boxes,
and there were bright flower beds in the square
gardens. All you could hear then was the clip-clop of
the passing carriages and the chirping of sparrows. It
must have been lovely—an Edwardian dream.

Three generations of Graces had their coming-out
balls in the long drawing room with French windows
overlooking the enclosed gardens of the square. The
last ball was in 1948 when my daughter, Dita, and I
went over for the coming-out party of my goddaughter,
Sally Hely-Hutchinson. As her father Ordy Donoughmore (my cousin) and I stood in the hall watching
the caterers scurrying around with tables and chairs,

From left, *Hubert Phipps, Winston and Raymond Guest, Peggie, Michael, and Ben Phipps, at Battle Abbey, c. 1911*

From left, *Elisa and Elena Grace, Grandpoods, Grandmoods, and Dita Grace, c. 1885*

and the florist and her helper arranging great vases of sweet peas, delphiniums, lupines, and roses that had been brought fresh from the country that morning, Ordy remarked to me, "This must be the most expensive way to make two little girls absolutely miserable and in tears." It was true. It all seemed too much for their vulnerable young hearts, though it was a lovely party.

When we were children, every summer we went abroad for the summer months to see Mother's family and for Father to have some shooting in Scotland. We never did any sightseeing because we were just visiting the family and doing what they did. We would first stay in London with Grandmoods. In the afternoons, she would go for a drive in her Rolls Royce. A liveried chauffeur and a footman sat in front; Grandmoods and Mrs. Gully, a sort of friend-cum-lady-in-waiting were seated in the back, with Joan Gully and me on the jump seats. Grandmoods was always very dressy which suited her.

Poor Grandmoods. Grandpoods had been engaged to her older sister who was known for her intelligence. When she died, Grandpoods transferred his affections to the younger sister, the beauty of the family. Unfortunately, she was never quite able to keep up with her husband's rapidly rising fortune, nor was she able to produce a male heir to carry on the Grace name. So she remained in the background, worrying about her four pretty daughters and fussing over her large households in London and the country. She irritated her daughters with constant admonishments.

*Grandmoods with her daughter Gladys,* left

Her youngest daughter, Gladys, told me that once when she and her mother were going up the Nile in a dahabiya, they hired a rower to take them ashore to see some ruins. Halfway across the river, Grandmoods noticed that Aunt Gladys had not brought along her galoshes. She insisted that they turn back to get them. The rower said, "Madame, it hasn't rained here for a thousand years." Nevertheless, they went back. I can understand how this characteristic maddened her husband and daughters, but none of this affected me. She spoiled us all; she sang funny little songs to us and recited rhymes. She had once seen a ghost that pointed to a hidden treasure, and I loved being in her house in London.

Whenever we left to go home to America she would say, "Kiss me goodby, darling, I may not be here when you come back next year." She was there for many, many years and it became a sort of family joke. I am sorry that I do not know more about her.

*With friends at Battle Abbey; Grandmoods,* seated left, *Grandpoods,* standing right, *and Dita,* center

*A house party at Battle Abbey:* seated, far left, *Aunt Gladys;* third from left, *Grandmoods;* far right, *Aunt Elisa;* standing far left, *Grandpoods;* fourth from left, *Uncle Hubert Beaumont*

*The Grace girls, c. 1890:* from left, *Gladys, Elena, Elisa, and Dita*

# RELATIONS

Gladys Grace, my favorite aunt, was born in 1888, twelve years younger than Mother and eighteen years older than I. As she lived to be ninety, we had plenty of time to reminisce about our past.

Her arrival as a fourth daughter was a great disappointment to her family. In fact, Grandpoods paid no attention to her at all until one day when she was about eight years old. He invited her to go for a walk with him, she accepted with alacrity, and, from then on, they were constant companions. It is sad to think of all the unwanted daughters whose lives were poisoned by the fact of their not being born males. It is only in the last few years that this passion for a son to carry on the name and fortune has disappeared.

My brother Michael once remarked, "Aunt Glad, you must have had a wonderful time when you were young—you are so pretty." To which she replied, "No. I was terribly shy. Moods, my mother, wouldn't let me go to school, so I stayed at home with a governess and I didn't know anybody. At my first ball, I stood in front of my mother all evening, and I only danced once with an old beau of your mother. As I hadn't been introduced to any young men, none of them dared to approach me."

The chaperones sat along the wall gossiping and enjoying themselves, while the debutantes stood in front of them and suffered agonies of embarrassment. Of course this situation didn't last long, but it left its mark. The following week, Aunt Glad "came out" at her own party, and after that she never lacked beaux.

One day her father said to her, "I've had a long conversation with your friend, Lord X. He told me that he was very fond of you but that he could not marry anyone with an income of less than fifty-thousand pounds a year, as it was his duty to keep up his estates and his title. I had to tell him that I couldn't afford to give you such a large dowry. I'm sorry because I like him very much." Aunt Glad laughed and said she had never had any intention of marrying him. Later Lord X did marry an American heiress who produced the dowry needed, and I believe they were very happy.

Among Aunt Gladys' many admirers was a distant cousin, Raymond Sheffield Hamilton Grace. He was charming and devoted and had proposed many times;

*Uncle Hubert Beaumont*

but as she was enjoying herself and in no hurry to get married, she refused him, and they stopped seeing each other. One day, on her way to London, she ran into him on the train, and they sat together in an empty compartment. In the course of conversation she asked, "Do you remember Robert X. He proposed to me at the party last night."

"And what did you say?"

"I told him that I couldn't accept him because I was already engaged to you!"

*A family performance of* The Pirates of Penzance: *Dita Grace is standing third from left; her sisters Elisa and Elena are seated center and far right.*

It was a blissful marriage but tragically short. Uncle Raymond was killed in the second year of the First World War. He left a small daughter and a son, born posthumously, who died as a child.

In later years, I would often stay with Aunt Glad in Frant, Sussex, in the spring when the woods were carpeted with bluebells and her lovely borders were in full bloom. We would sit in the garden or by the fire, according to the weather, and talk endlessly of my generation or of hers. However, her favorite visitor was my brother Michael. He would take her to the races, and they would discuss the merits of their racehorses nonstop.

Through the years, she had won several gold or silver trophies which were displayed on a table in the library. When her second husband, Uncle Josh, died and there was only herself and two ancient maids sleeping in the house, each night the gold cups were carried up and hidden under her bed, to be guarded by Col, her Highland terrier, who would have gladly attacked the burglars or anyone else.

Col, the terrier, was a menace. It was impossible to stay in the house for more than a few hours without being bitten. For no reason at all, he would just come up to you and bite you. This disagreeable habit was most awkward when visitors came to tea, or the doctors and nurses tried to be helpful. I protected myself by slipping him tidbits and chocolates. I decided that it was better for him to have indigestion than for me to be bitten, even though the maids let me know their displeasure at my sneaky behavior.

When Aunt Glad was very old and fairly blind, she would lean on my arm as we walked slowly down her herbaceous garden admiring the glorious display of color and discussing the merits of the various plants. Seeing a small flower whose name I didn't know, I asked, "What is that little yellow one? I have never seen it before." To which she answered, "I can't tell you. You see, I don't really see the flowers any more. I just know where they are, and I can picture it all when you tell me what is in bloom."

And in 1978, she went to her rest in the lovely little graveyard of the church in her village. Near her are the graves of her husband Raymond Hamilton Grace, her son Raymond Hamilton Grace, and her grandson Raymond.

*Aunt Gladys Grace*

*Uncle Raymond Hamilton Grace*

*Aunt Elena, age fourteen*

My mother's sister, Elena, married Viscount Suirdale, son of the Earl of Donoughmore, Grandpoods' partner in the Chilean railroad venture. When the Graces moved to London, it was arranged that the three Grace sisters were to be introduced to society and presented at court by the Dowager Countess of Donoughmore.

Uncle Suirdale and Aunt Lin divided their time between London, Sussex, and County Tipperary. The fact that my aunt was considered an American and also that she had been so generous to the poor saved their place from being burned down by the Sinn Fein. This has been the sad fate of so many English-Irish estates. Eamon de Valera, who later became the first president of the Irish Republic, occupied their house, Knocklofty, for a short while with his revolutionary followers. Nothing was damaged, and he wrote a polite note of thanks in the guest book before leaving.

We had many cousins on both sides of the Atlantic. We were really brought up with all of them and were devoted to them. All of Mother's nieces and nephews stayed with us in Westbury for many months

From left, *Elena, Dita, and Elisa Grace with their cousins, the daughters of William Russell Grace*

and even years, so they do have a definite part in the annals of Westbury House.

Aunt Elena's son, Lord Donoughmore, my cousin Ordy, and his beautiful wife, Jeanie, were everyone's favorites. They lived in London until after the Second World War, when they moved to Ireland. Their ancestral home, Knocklofty, became, like Westbury, a happy center for all the family. Ordy wrote to me about our times together at Westbury House:

> In 1928 Jeanie and I, with Michael, then a year old, went to America for me to work with the W. R. Grace Company. We meant to find an apartment in New York but, in fact, stayed at Westbury for nine months and then moved to the Phipps' apartment in Sutton Place for the three months of the winter. By the time I was sent back to the London office, our very kind Phipps aunt, uncle, and cousins had more or less adopted us into the family. From then on, we looked upon Westbury as our American home, and Aunt Dita as a second mother. We

will never forget those happy times, and the closeness formed between the Irish and American cousins has remained the same to this day.

> In 1940, just after Hitler's invasion of France, a cable arrived from Uncle Jay in New York to my mother, inviting her to send her family and friends to be guests in America for the duration of the war. This wonderful offer was accepted, and about forty children and a few parents set sail in June 1940. For over three years, our three children lived at Westbury House and were cared for in every way, with all the love and attention possible. So, another generation of the Irish/English family also had the benefit of knowing and growing up in Westbury, coming to feel as we had that Westbury was their home too.

Ordy and Jeanie had the terrifying experience of being kidnapped by the Irish Republican Army. By happenstance I arrived in England the day of the kidnapping. As I walked in the front door of my Aunt Gladys' house, I was greeted by the two maids with,

"Have you heard about Lord and Lady Donoughmore?"

"No," I said, "what about them?"

"They have been kidnapped by the I.R.A., and we don't know where they are or if they are alive or dead."

It was unbelievable. We started to live a long nightmare. Being an optimist, I thought that eventually things would turn out all right, but that thought was only a thin lifeline to cling to among all the fears and rumors that surrounded us. We sat by the television all day, listening to an extravagant jumble of facts and fancies. Finally Aunt Glad and I took to the garden where from time to time Katherine or Violet would rush out of the house to tell us that they were dragging the Suir River or searching for bodies in the woods.

Ordy had been a Member of Parliament, and, as he later wrote to me,

> Our captors thought they could use me to talk to the Labour Home Secretary in an effort to let five people (two of them were girls), who were on a hunger strike in various British prisons, serve the balance of their sentences in Ireland. In fact, this never arose because the hunger strikers (all of them I think were murderers) had already been told they might serve the remainder of their sentences in Northern Ireland.
>
> The kidnapping was certainly a traumatic event for us. We were returning from having dinner with neighbors at about 11:00 P.M. when Jeanie noticed that we were being followed. Outside the front door were four masked men with guns who seized us, bundled us into a car, and drove off. All this not without a fight. I was hit on the head several times, Jeanie fought and hit her captor, but we were in no position to win, and in a short time, we were pushed into the car and were blindfolded with sticky tape. After what seemed hours, we were moved out of the first car and eventually into another and finally a third one and driven to an unknown destination (probably a small house or bungalow) where we were held and guarded for four days and five nights.

Those days were ones of fear and misery for us too. On the third day, Ordy's small hometown of Clonmel organized a gathering of Catholics and Protestants. The crowds filled the church and spilled out onto the streets and sidewalks even though everyone knew that the I.R.A. was watching to see who was attending. More than twelve hundred people came to pray for the safe return of the Donoughmores and to petition the kidnappers to take good care of the two elderly and much loved members of their town.

*Aunt Elena, the Countess of Donoughmore*

Late on the fourth night, one of the guards woke their hostages to say, "The girls (in prison) have taken some tea; you will be released."

Ordy sprang out of bed saying, "Okay, let's go." He was told that they would leave before dawn, when they were put back in the car, this time with a handkerchief over their eyes. They drove for about two hours, then when they approached Dublin, they were told to take off their blindfolds but to keep their eyes down as their captors would have to unmask to pass through one of the checkpoints surrounding the city. They passed without incident, obviously by previous arrangement, and drove to Phoenix Park where they were left by the side of the road.

As they stood, free in the early dawn, a stag with beautiful wide antlers appeared through the mist, gazed at them, and wandered off. Soon they found a police booth, knocked on the door and told the guardian, "We are Lord and Lady Donoughmore. Will you take us to a telephone?"

The policeman just stared at them. "Well," he

said at last, "you couldn't have told me better news if you'd told me I'd won the Irish Sweepstakes."

The following week, Etienne and I went to Knocklofty. There were wounds on Ordy's head where he had been beaten with a pistol, and one side of Jeanie's face was badly bruised from the blow she had received from the leader of the group. At their first stop, as she lay on the ground waiting to be changed from one car to another, she complained that she felt sick. Her assailant remarked, "You wouldn't be feeling that way if you hadn't fought and bitten me." To which Jeanie answered, "What would you have done if you had been me?"

He replied, "I suppose the same thing."

Jeanie's great terror had been that she and Ordy would be separated, but they shared one small room and single bed for the whole of their captivity. Even though their ordeal ended happily, and Ordy later described it as being simply "fairly frightening and incredibly boring," still, to be cooped up in one small room with the blinds drawn and a masked man constantly with you was a horrifying experience that took its toll on their health and well-being.

My mother's eldest sister, Elisa, married Hubert Beaumont, a most aristocratic-looking man. In fact, Uncle Hubert so resembled Edward VI that his car was often mistakenly allowed to pass through the traffic by a patriotic policeman. He was not treated so royally on this side of the Atlantic. One year on his arrival in New York to visit my family, he was asked by the customs officer if he was for overthrowing the United States government, to which he answered emphatically, "Yes. Yes, of course, I am. 100 percent for it." He was taken to Ellis Island where he spent an uncomfortable night. Next morning after a lot of string pulling, Father was able to have him released and to bring him back to the mainland.

Uncle Hubert and Aunt Lise lived in a beautiful Queen Anne house not far from Oxford. On a holiday in Switzerland, they went out sailing with their son. A sudden storm capsized their boat. Uncle Hubert saved their little boy, Michael, but when he turned around for his wife, she was gone. He never married again.

Michael Beaumont was the same age as Ben and Ordy Suirdale, and though he played all our games, he seemed to belong to an earlier era. When England became too socialistic or democratic for his taste, he took on Irish citizenship, and he and his Irish wife moved to a house in Harristown near Dublin. In this more feudal country, he lived happily. He was Master of the Hunt and won many prizes at the Dublin Horse Show.

There is no doubt that Aunt Amy Phipps Guest was the most original and imaginative member of our family. I always thought that she should have been a man—she was so forceful and so absolutely fearless. I have seen her riding sidesaddle on a borrowed horse, suddenly turning away from the rest of the hunt and urging her horse over an enormous fence taken at short range.

As a young woman, she launched the family into a society that was compatible with their growing fortune. She married Freddy Guest, son of Lord Wynbourne and first cousin to Winston Churchill. By the time I remember Aunt Amy, Father was the accepted head of the family, but Aunt Amy often came to the house both to give him advice and to ask his opinion on her various projects. The sister and brother were alike—in their robust looks and their equally robust characters. Father told me that poor Amy had always been thwarted in her attempts to be of help to mankind. During the Spanish American War she wanted to go to Mexico to nurse the wounded. Grandpa asked her, "Do you want to help our soldiers or do you just want to go out there personally, because if you really want to help the wounded, your mother and I will pay for two trained nurses to work at the army hospital for the duration of the war." What could she say!

Soon after Lindbergh's flight across the ocean, there was a rumor that Rosa Lewis, a nightclub hostess, was planning to be the first woman to fly the Atlantic. Aunt Amy quite rightly did not approve of a nightclub hostess representing the United States, so she decided to get a plane and pilot and be the first woman herself. There are several different versions of the story, but the one I heard was that she did not tell the family about the trip, with the exception of her youngest brother, Howard, and she swore him to secrecy. As the time for the flight neared, Howard became more and more worried and finally he broke down, called up Winston (Guest), and spilled the beans. Winston then phoned his mother from Yale and said definitely, "No—the day you get on the plane, I will leave college." So again, Aunt Amy had to give up her plans. She generously arranged to have Amelia Earhart take her place. Of course, this was more practical, for not only did Amelia know how to fly, but she also weighed very little. However, Aunt Amy was definitely a great help to her husband's country, England, and to mankind in general. I wonder if she realized the importance of her contribution to the 1939 war effort. In the early thirties, she heavily financed the Supermarine Aviation Company, making it possible for its factories to turn out hundreds of planes before the war. It was the Spitfires and other Supermarines with their fantastic young pilots that

*Ordy and Jeanie Suirdale on their wedding day*

*Aunt Amy, always poised*

*Cousin Michael Beaumont accepting a trophy from Queen Elizabeth at the Dublin Horse Show*

chased the Luftwaffe from the skies and won the Battle of Britain.

One spring, Aunt Amy took her daughter Diana and me on a trip to Italy. I joined them from Oxford, and it wasn't till we were on the Channel boat that I discovered that I had forgotten my passport. Following closely in Aunt Amy's footsteps, I went through France and Switzerland with no trouble at all, and then early in the morning at Domodossola, we woke to find two Italian custom officers at our door demanding my passport. There was general confusion. Diana was sneezing nonstop from an attack of hay fever, and I was trying desperately to get dressed and stay safely in the compartment till Aunt Amy came to the rescue. She arrived smiling her Christian Science smile but ready to do battle. She had flung her skunk-skin coat over her nightgown, and she was both a majestic and a formidable figure. She explained to the officers that her husband was an important member of the British Parliament and that he had already arranged to have my passport sent to Rome to the attention of Mussolini. The guards were not impressed and became quite rude. One grabbed my arm and said, "I will take care of her." Aunt Amy took my other arm and held it firmly. It was finally agreed that we would all three get off the train and go to a hotel to telephone Rome for a pass. The guards were highly skeptical and annoyingly amused. An official pass arrived next morning, and we sailed past the customs with our noses in the air. Aunt Amy never mentioned the inconvenience of my having forgotten my passport.

We "did" Rome and went south to stay in Capri. Many years before, Grandma and Grandpa Phipps had known the famous Axel Munte, and he had been in love with Aunt Amy. One morning we drove up to his house in Anacapri, rang the bell, and walked in past the butler who tried to explain that the "princess" was at lunch. So she was! Although we never did discover exactly who she was, we found her entertaining a small luncheon party. We circled the table with Aunt Amy bowing graciously to the astonished guests. Diana and I crept behind her, overcome with embarrassment. Then we inspected the rest of the house. The princess and her guests had tactfully disappeared.

Father and Aunt Amy never let barriers or "no-trespassing" signs deter them. It wasn't that they consciously broke the law, it was just that they did not think that the law applied to them. They were special people.

Clockwise, from left, *Aunt Amy (Mrs. Frederick Guest), Bradley Martin, his sister Cornelia Lady Craven*, Lord Craven (seated), *and Aunt Helen Phipps (Mrs. Bradley Martin)*

*The terrace at Westbury House, view from above and down the south allée*

Westbury House was home to all of us. Though we went to Palm Beach every winter and spent part of the summer in England, Scotland, Canada, or New England, it was at Westbury that we had our roots and grew up.

The red brick house sits on a slight rise in the middle of the property. Long avenues of beech and linden trees lead up to it from the north and south, while on either side are large ornamental lakes. The surrounding lanes and avenues open onto a natural landscape of woods and meadows forming a "picture garden" in the marvelously harmonious style of an eighteenth-century English country park.

The house was usually full with the family and visiting cousins and friends. Each of us owned a dog, and Grandpoods had a gray parrot and a macaw that perched in the dining room. Everything that one could possibly want was to be found on the place. There was a large stable for ponies, hunters, polo ponies, and, later, racehorses. Adjoining the stables was a kennel for Father's beagles. Our neighbors, the Thomas Hitchcocks, also had a pack of beagles, and we would join forces on a hunt.

The boys did quite a lot of fishing in the lake and pond for sunfish or perch. Occasionally, we swam in the lake, but the bottom was muddy, and repulsive leeches were apt to attach themselves to our legs, so we were glad when the pool was built. Between the lake and the polo field there was a nine-hole golf course made especially for Grandpoods. A flock of sheep kept the grass down until one night a pack of dogs attacked them and killed some of the ewes. As we were acquiring new neighbors with dogs, it became impossible to protect the flock, and the golf course was reluctantly abandoned. We had two grass tennis courts and a wooden court with a canvas over it that eventually became an indoor tennis court.

On one corner of the place, there was a large farm that provided us with fresh butter and thick cream and also with another form of amusement: climbing into the paddock where the bull was kept. We circled round at a distance trying to annoy him into chasing us. As I was the only one who owned a red sweater, I was supposed to be the lure. Owing to the fact that I had an extremely timid nature and bulls are colorblind, this game did not last very long.

*Michael,* top, *Hubert, and the Sphinx, Westbury House*

Mother's greatest pleasure was in the gardens—the circular Rose Garden which was copied from one at Battle Abbey and the Walled Garden which also followed the plans of the typical English gardens. In the thirty herbaceous borders grew a profusion of all the lovely hardy plants—Delphinium, phlox, lilies, Michaelmas daisies, lavender, tulips, and pansies. There were espaliered fruit trees and clematis against the pale brick walls, and pink pillar roses clung to the chains lining the paths. The beds of the Rose Garden were bordered with boxwood and filled with a great variety of tea roses. Beyond were the green-

*Westbury House viewed from the west pond, c. 1910*

houses and vegetable gardens. Keeping everything in beautiful order, there were about thirty gardeners.

Though all the seasons on Long Island had their charm, I think October was our favorite month. We rode our ponies all over the place. There were few cars, and all the neighbors were our friends. The boys would fish in the pond and get up early in the morning to trap muskrats to sell their fur—who bought them I can't imagine. When the cornstalks were gathered in the fields, again it was the boys and their friends who brought their dogs for a great rat hunt. In the woods were wild grapevines which we used for swings, or we would climb on the trellis in the Walled Garden to eat Concord grapes whose heavy skins contained a sweet flavor that is the very essence of an American fall.

In the years between the two world wars, the Piping Rock Horse Show was a great attraction. Held in September or October in a large field near the club, it was a showcase for hunters, jumpers, and ponies of all sorts. It also gave us a happy excuse to indulge in smart new autumn clothes. We mostly bought from Bendel's, DePinna, Bonwit Teller, Lord and Taylors, Best and Taffe—and later from Hattie Carnegie and Bergdorf Goodman. Sometimes we would bring back a dress from Paris, but that was rare.

*On the terrace, from left, Hubert, Peggie, and Ben, c. 1913*

In later autumn, we would gather nuts from the chestnut trees that grew so luxuriously all over the island in earlier days, and in the evenings, we roasted them by the fire while listening to *A Christmas Carol* and other winter tales. The Christmas season gave me a much needed respite from our usual evening reading of *Drake and His Yeomen* or horrifying Indian stories. These bloody tales of autos-da-fé—burnings at the stake—chosen by the boys gave me nightmares. My only comfort was that they took place way in the past—now I wonder!

In those days, winter seemed to come earlier and last longer than now. Soon after Thanksgiving, the snow fell and we went sleighing on the Roslyn hills and skating on the ponds. The spirit of Christmas followed in due course. It was a season of magic excitement. We knew that Santa Claus and his little men were working away somewhere near the North Pole making toys for children—and we were busy ourselves, sewing and painting presents for the family.

Christmas Eve we hung our stockings on the mantlepiece in Mother's and Father's room, and then, promising not to come down till seven o'clock next morning, we went reluctantly to bed. When we woke up, we each found a present by our pillows to while away the time. Then, at the appointed moment, we tore downstairs and rushed into Mother's room where everybody hugged everybody and wished them a Merry Christmas.

The stockings were just where we had left them the night before, but now, instead of hanging limply, they were fat and bulging with presents, candy sticks, and wooly animals; bright packages filled the tops, and in each of the toes there was a twenty-dollar gold piece. The boys' stockings contained all those things that boys want, and by my stocking one Christmas was a beautiful doll. She was almost as big as I was. She had curly brown hair and pink cheeks, and her china eyes were very blue. She wore a dress made of linen and Irish lace with a pink sash, just like the

*Children playing on the South Lawn*

*Hubert*

*Peggie and Fay*

*Peggie with Grandpoods' parrot*

*Michael in the garden beds, c. 1913*

one I wore for dancing class. She was the answer to my dreams, and the fact that a week before, snooping around the house, I had come upon that same dress in the pressing room did not make me any less grateful to Santa Claus for my presents.

After church we were joined by some of our cousins for Christmas lunch, an enormous turkey with all the trimmings, followed by ice cream, and plum pudding. We teased each other about who would get which favor in their helping of pudding—they

*On the garden swing, c. 1913*

*Hubert*

*Hubert and Peggie on the drive*

consisted of a thimble for the old maid, an engagement ring, a baby, and a quarter for the future millionaire. Of course, they all went to the wrong people—a spinster or some little boy would be left holding the baby.

Then it was time for our tree. It stood tall and beautiful in the red drawing room, sparkling with Christmas ornaments and real candles, with brightly colored packages piled around its base. There were presents for everyone in the house including the

*The stables, Westbury*

*Jay*

*Dita with Peggie*

*Hubert*

*Michael*

*The Westbury beagle pack, c. 1918*

dogs. Here was the pleasure of giving as well as receiving. Cross-stitched handkerchiefs, carefully colored cards, and clay ashtrays in the form of animals were unwrapped and admired as we looked on proudly at our handiwork.

As I was the oldest girl in a predominantly male family, I received many exciting gifts. One Christmas Mother made me a dish garden with a tiny pool and a mossy bank for Titania and her fairy band.

Later in the afternoon, we bundled into a large

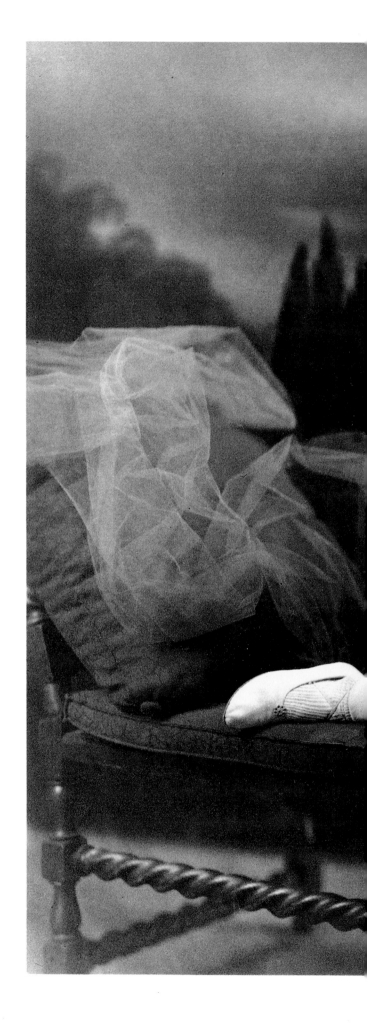

*Peggie with miniature figures of Queen Titania and her court, Christmas, 1912*

*Peggie with her Christmas doll, dressed alike*

*In the Walled Garden*

*Hubert poised to take aim, the west pond, 1914*

sleigh pulled by one of the horses. We trotted down our drive, around the Old Westbury pond, gay with skaters, and up the hill to Aunt Helen Martin's. The whole family was gathered there—Grandma Phipps, uncles, aunts, and cousins. A few very special presents were exchanged, then the youngsters played while the grownups had tea. The moon came out, the sleigh waited for us at the front door, and we drove peace-fully home to dream of our lovely day.

The winters were too long and, even as it is today, there was always someone with a bad cold which would be passed around to the whole house-hold. Without our modern drugs, sore throats could become infected, and earaches were dreaded, as the eardrums often had to be lanced. When Hubert was about seven, he had a mastoid operation which was

*Westbury House: the second-floor landing, where the wind wailed like banshees through the window panes*

*Cousin Ogden Phipps on the lake, c. 1917*

*Michael, ice sailing on the lake, 1914*

a nightmare for him and for all of us. We were always sent outdoors when the doctors came, but we knew how much he suffered with the painful dressings. After tetracycline was discovered and during the four war years when I worked in various hospitals, I saw only one case of mastoids, and not surprisingly it was a small boy. Thanks to antibiotics, the day after the operation, he was bouncing on his bed, squealing with delight, and insisting that I carry him around to show off his bandaged head to the other children.

Though colds were a misery and a bore, they were also a rest from everyday living. In my room with all my favorite books, I could dream the time away, transported to a world of romance and adventure; and if my temperature rose and there was a ringing in my ears, it came from the bell of a little man at the gates selling roasted chestnuts. I loved the little man who wasn't there.

While Westbury House was being built, we had an oak branch nailed across the front door, as either Mr. Crawley or the builder was rather superstitious, and so there were no accidents and consequently no ghosts. There may not have been phantoms in the house, but, on the second floor at the top of the stairs, there is a north window which moans and groans when the wind blows. As we all had to go to bed according to age, each of us had to pass this window alone. One of my cousins thought the weird noises were made by suffragettes who, we were told, played violins in a certain way to shatter the panes of glass. He slept with a penknife under his pillow. I was afraid it was a giant peering in the window. I

*Peggie and Hubert taking an ice-skating lesson, c. 1914*

*The Meadow Brook Hunt, Westbury, c. 1925*

*Peggie Phipps Douglas on Rhonny at the Orange County Hunt, Virginia, 1936*

remember assuring Mother that I certainly did not believe in giants, then pleading that there just might be one left. Anyhow, to be on the safe side, we all raced through the hall to the third floor and the shelter of our beds.

Quite soon after the family moved into Westbury, we found that things began to disappear—a silver brush, some rather valuable ornaments, and some of Father's silk shirts. Several times footsteps were heard in the early hours of the morning. Father would rush out in his nightshirt to catch the burglar and instead find the butler, armed with a flashlight, already searching the rooms. "I thought I heard footsteps, Mr. Phipps, so I ran upstairs." They went through all the rooms together and found nothing. This happened two or three times until it finally dawned on Father that the butler and the burglar were one and the same person.

Some of the visitors to the Old Westbury Gardens may have noticed that in the passage going to the best guestroom there is a plain white wooden cupboard with a small metal box projecting from one side. This was where the night watchman used to turn his key each time he made his rounds from 10:00 P.M. to 6:00 A.M. (This device must have been installed after the above story but abandoned before the time of our second intruder described earlier in Ben's story.)

Until we were thirteen, twelve, and eleven years of age respectively, Ben, Hubert, and I went to St. Bernard's in the village and then to day schools in New York, but there were always long weekends at home. The Christmas holidays were spent at Westbury and, later on, the Easter holidays in Palm Beach. Spring was the time for picking flowers and looking forward to the long summer vacations.

*The Meadow Brook Hunt*

*The Meadow Brook Hunt in winter, c. 1925*

*The wheeled chair and driver, Palm Beach, c. 1914:* from left, *Hubert, Michael, Peggie, and Ben*

Our first winters in Palm Beach were spent with Grandpoods in his rented cottage, the Oceanic. It was one of the Breakers' beach cottages—a large, square, shingled house, standing in a row of identical houses. The front porch faced the ocean, and the two sides gave onto the hotel golf course. There were no automobiles at all on Palm Beach Island until after the First World War—not even one road for cars. Instead there was a path connecting the Breakers on the ocean and the Poincianna on the lake, and over this we rode on bicycles, wheelchairs, and buckboards run with Smith motor wheels. The wheelchairs were made of wicker and would seat two large or three small people. Our wheelchair man was a tall and handsome black man, and we loved him dearly. He was especially kind to us children.

Also going north and south between the Breakers and the Poincianna was a small trolley line. The trolley was miniature, holding only about eight people, and was pulled by a donkey. Eventually, there was a road for deliveries. It ran in back of the houses and then rejoined the only other road on the main island on which cars were allowed. At one point, this road cut across the old wheelchair and bicycle path. A man on duty at the intersection of these two thoroughfares directed traffic—in other words, seeing to it that the cars and trolley stopped politely to let the pedestrians, bicyclists, golfers, and wheelchairs go by.

In the evenings, we played games on the golf course, and the boys caught fireflies—to put in my hair. There was a small woods on one side of the course in which we used to explore by cutting trails through the underbrush with Ben's hatchet. At that time, the Florida wildlife was very much a part of Palm Beach. There was an alligator farm in West Palm Beach which we used to visit. When we were older and went on picnics up the Loxahatchee River, we would see these long, ugly beasts go slithering off the banks into the water. One day Ben caught three baby alligators which we took home as pets. They were not very affectionate, but when we tickled their tummies to mesmerize them, they would give little squeaky grunts and roll their eyes in an ecstatic manner. There was also a man who would come to the house with a bag of rattlesnakes; he showed them off by letting them crawl over him and sometimes even teasing them. He said that he had been bitten often and was immune to their poison. One day this proved not to be true, and he died of a snake bite.

Several years after our first Florida winter, the family bought a tract of land a bit north of the Breakers where all the houses had large gardens and private beaches. This acreage was divided between my father, the Hal Phippses, and Michael Grace. Aunt Amy was just down the road.

Our house, Casa Bendita, was designed by

Addison Mizner in the Spanish style that he used for all his Palm Beach houses. I don't know if the weather has become colder or the draining of the Everglades has made the air dryer and cooler, but when Casa Bendita was built (1924–26), there was no central heating, and the loggia, corridors, and stairs were all open to the air. The gardens seemed part of the house, with white butterfly orchids and gardenias flanking the steps going from the front door. Purple bougainvillea, and yellow allamanda climbed over the walls and the colonnades that formed the patio.

There were two swimming pools, one of which was under our bedroom wing. There were arches on three sides of the pool supporting the second floor but still leaving the pool half in the garden and half in the house. There was a larger pool, made of coral or Florida Keys' stone, in the garden by the tennis court. At intervals along the pool's sides were antique urns filled to overflowing with orange and yellow nasturtiums. At the back, there was a higher wall also of coral with sculptured heads from whose mouths water gushed to fill the pool.

*The ferry that connected Palm Beach with West Palm Beach*

*Palm Beach—transporting the canoe for an outing and alligator hunt in the Everglades*

219

*Hubert and Peggie at Palm Beach, c. 1908*

*Ben, Hubert, and Peggie with Captain Grey*

From left, *Malcolm Chace, Jr., Winston Guest, Hubert, Peggie, Eliot Chace, and Raymond Guest, Palm Beach, c. 1914*

*On the beach outside the Breakers Hotel, Palm Beach, c. 1911*

*Discovering a giant sea turtle, Palm Beach, c. 1911*

*Peggie*

*Ogden Phipps flanked by two giant tarpon, aboard the* Seminole

I was describing Palm Beach to my oldest grandson, and he remarked in a rather shocked voice, "Grandma, didn't you ever think of your grandfathers who worked so hard to give you all these luxuries—" I had to answer, "No, I don't think I ever did." We were the third generation living in an affluent era. Most of our friends seemed rich or rich enough, and of course all our aunts and uncles had places just like ours. In those days, charities were personal and emotional. I remember crying myself into a fever when I read about vivisection and weeping sentimentally over "The Little Match Girl" and "Baa-Baa Black Sheep" by Kipling. And I did vaguely plan to buy warm blankets for the poor when I was older and had some money. Later, when the graduated income tax was passed, I found it eminently fair—just as I do the Social Security System—but these humanitarian ideas were all in the future when we were young.

When Palm Beach started to become more fashionable, Mother and Father retired more and more into their own surroundings. However, this did not make for a lonely life because every winter there were long visits from members of Mother's family and plenty of the younger generation to enjoy the tennis, golf, and fishing, with occasional parties at friends' houses, the Everglades Club, or the Bath and Tennis Club.

As children, we would swim and play on the beach much as we did during the summers on Long Island. When we stopped building sandcastles and were at schools or college, we came down with friends to play games and fool around in the glorious weather. However, with the exception of Michael and Molly, none of us ever became part of the Palm Beach scene.

I don't suppose there was any little girl who was more spoiled than I was in the way of being given presents. Yet, I vividly remember an incident which happened one winter when we were living in Palm Beach. I must have been eight or nine and my passion in life was paper dolls.

Every once in a while, we would go from Palm

Left: *Shipboard activity—someone was pushed.*
Below: *The Phipps houseboat, the* Seminole, *in the Florida Keys, c. 1916*

*Grandpoods and Hubert with a sailfish, Los Incas, Palm Beach, c. 1914*

Beach to West Palm Beach to do some shopping. This was quite an expedition and a great treat. Sometimes we went by ferry. The drawbridge between the two Palm Beaches often had to be opened for boats, a procedure that took a lot of time, and even in those days, there was a fair amount of marine traffic. Whenever a boat going to the inlet or the inland waterways wanted to pass through the bridge, it would toot its horn well before arrival, gates would be closed at both ends of the bridge, and a man would come out of a small shelter in the middle and start turning the turnstile by pushing a long pole around and around. The gateway would swing open, the boat or maybe two would go by, then the same maneuver would be used to close the bridge. As this caused long delays, the ferry was the easiest way to cross the lake and more fun.

One day Mother and Grandpoods decided to take us to West Palm on a shopping spree. Naturally, our first visit was to Palm Beach Mercantile Company for fishing tackle for the boys and then to the drugstore for ice-cream sodas, and we would wind up at the toy store. On an earlier visit, I had seen a paper doll in the toy shop window. It was a little black girl paper doll rather larger than usual, with dresses made of printed cotton instead of paper. I longed for her, but I was too young to have an allowance so I couldn't buy her. As we went into the toy shop, Grandpoods said, "I want to give you a present. Choose anything you want." My heart stopped—I wanted the doll so much yet I just couldn't ask for her or even look at her. In my confusion and misery, I brusquely turned down the various toys that were offered to me. Afterwards Mother scolded me, "How could you have

*Part of the day's catch:* from left, *Ben, Peggie, Ogden, Michael, and Hubert*

*The Phipps' Palm Beach residence, Casa Bendita, Addison Mizner, architect*

*The sun room, Casa Bendita*

acted like that—Grandpoods was looking forward to giving you a present. Surely you could have just picked out something to give him pleasure." I still remember that day with sadness and regret. Why does human nature have to be so terribly difficult and complicated?

For several years, we had a houseboat tied up to the dock in Palm Beach. It was a great big comfortable tub. During the winter, it was used for short excursions; in August, we would take it down to the Keys and fish for tarpon and bonefish. I especially remember one summer on the houseboat. In July there had been a dancing class at Westbury. The three Guest cousins seemed to be coughing a lot for that time of year, so Mother suggested that perhaps they had something that was catching and shouldn't be around the other children. Aunt Amy, who was an ardent Christian Scientist, insisted that there was nothing wrong. The result was that the whole class got the whooping cough. It was decided to take the three Guest children and the four of us to the Keys where the hot sun and the sea breeze would soon cure our coughs.

Hubert was the fisherman of our family, and I was the nonfisherman, but to troll for tarpon on a moonlit night and to watch the bonefish fins as they circled around in the shallow water approaching your bait was a delight for anyone. We children speared crawfish with a gig, and once while I was in the shallows, Winston was chasing a small shark nearby. In the excitement, it swam right at me and knocked me down. I suppose we were equally frightened. Captain Grey, our private fisherman and our hero, would slide his bare hand under the rocks and pull out a stone crab, whose claw has no rival in the shellfish world. At one time, they were so sought after that the crabs almost became extinct. Then a law was passed that only one claw should be taken off and the crab released at once to grow its new claw. Strangely enough, the law has been obeyed, and the crab population has flourished.

We swam every day in a natural pool of water protected from the sea by a net at its mouth. One year, after we left, someone wanted to deepen the pool, so they blasted it , and to everyone's shock, an enormous shark was blown to the surface.

*The covered pool, Casa Bendita*

Before and after the First World War, we would go every summer to stay with Grandpoods and Grandmoods in England and Scotland. Since we could not go abroad during the war, the family rented a fishing camp on the Cascapedia River in Quebec. It was a small red farmhouse right by the river. We slept outside, in beds with mosquito netting tented over them like little rooms. Every day we would fish from canoes up and down the river, and when we had enough trout, we would paddle ashore to a rocky beach and put the fish in a frying pan with a rasher of bacon and grill them over an open fire.

Once we went up the river for several miles and then drove inland in a logging wagon to a camp by a lake. The lake was supposed to be full of trout, and we had counted on them for a large part of our menu. That year the fishing was not good, and we were quite hungry. It was just such an expedition that made us feel that we were pioneering Americans. One night we heard a slow and heavy step on the porch, and looking out, we saw a large porcupine. They caused us a lot of trouble, for the dogs would not leave them alone. Always getting the worst of the encounter, they would come limping home covered with barbed quills, their noses like pin cushions. Unfortunately, the dogs also used to get tangled with skunks.

*A summer cookout, Quebec, 1915:* from left, *Dita, Michael, Ben, Hubert, and Peggie*

*Red Camp, the Phipps cabin in Quebec, Canada, c. 1915*

*Swimming in the Cascapedia River, Quebec, c. 1915*

*Hubert with his prize, c. 1915*

Later, the combined family bought a stretch of the river and built two camps. We had a one-third share of the lower one, Camp Chaleur. It was on a bluff overlooking the best salmon pool. Built in the style of a log cabin, of rough logs, each bedroom had its own fireplace and a door going onto an open corridor. There was a large sitting room, with red curtains and a fireplace made for six-foot logs, and a dining room where we ate mountains of pancakes with maple syrup. The cook and the guides were of Irish or Scottish descent, and what a hard-working, jovial lot they were. In the summer, acting as guides was easy work, but to make a living in the winter, they had to haul logs in below-zero weather. When they got older they had a hard time of it, and sometimes one of them would ask Father to help him through the difficult months.

*Ben and Michael, hiking in Scotland, 1921*

For many years, we visited Grandmoods in England or Grandpoods in Scotland. For two summers, Grandpoods rented Cortegie Castle in the lowlands of Scotland and invited us all to stay with him. There is a legend in the family of Lord Ailie, the owner, that when the son and heir dies drums are heard in the castle tower. During the Boer War, a young houseguest complained at breakfast that he had been unable to sleep all night because of the sounds of drums coming from the tower room above his head. Lady Ailie fainted. Two days later, she received word that her oldest son had been killed in battle. Nothing so dramatic happened while we were there. However, many years later during the Second World War, I met an officer at a U.S.O. party who told me that he had been sent to a Scottish castle which had been used as a hospital. One night he too had been disturbed by the beating of drums coming from the room above him. He was warned not to mention this to his hosts; and as he was sent home to America shortly after, we never knew the end of the story. He couldn't recall the name of the castle, but when I mentioned Cortegie, he said, "Yes, of course, that's where I was."

After Grandpoods died, it was our family who rented a shooting lodge in Scotland—Ardveriky in Inverness—and invited all Mother's relatives to stay with us. We would be eighteen or twenty at table. The shooting season was about six weeks, beginning in August with the grouse shooting and ending with the deer season in late September. Sometimes the shooters would walk over the moors in a line, and the birds would break cover and fly out in front of them. Each "gun" had a dog who would retrieve the birds shot by his master. On other days we would stand in the butts and beaters would walk up the hill towards us, beating the heather and calling out. I never could learn to shoot, but when there was a drive I loaded for Ben. He would fire one of his double-barreled guns, give it to me with his left hand, and I would pass him the second gun to his right, losing no time in the transaction. The "guns" were always competitive about the number of grouse they killed, so it was exciting. A good loader was a help, and so was a smart dog, who would occasionally pick up a neighbor's grouse. Around noon the lunch would arrive, and we would sit in the heather and eat hot mincemeat pies and other tasty picnic fare.

Like many Scottish houses, Ardveriky was made of gray granite, with many towers, in the Victorian fortress style. The view of the loch was ever charming and glorious. A bed of orange tiger lilies grew by the wharf, bringing a bright note to a world of misty purples and blues.

After coming in from shooting, we dined at a late hour because we all had to take turns at the bathrooms, which were grouped together at the end of a long corridor. It was thwarting to hurry out in your dressing gown, ready with towels and sponge, only to find someone else standing at the bathroom door before you or an earlier arrival singing in the bathtub. And the "W.C." was a worse problem!

After dinner we would play rowdy games like "Sardines" or "thirteen chairs." The year Aunt Glad married a cocky young major whom the boys didn't like, these games gave ample scope to give our new uncle a rough time. Father and Uncle Suirdale didn't approve of their new relative either, so during his visit they dined in the library. Poor Uncle Josh must have thought us a very peculiar family.

*Ardveriky, Inverness, Scotland*

*Stopping for tea on the moors, Scotland, 1921*

233

Right: *Jay and Michael, 1921*

*Michael picnicking on a Scottish moor, 1921*

*The old mill in Middleburg—Jay's Virginia house*

One reason that the family had so many homes was that whenever one of the children moved to a new place, Mother and Father would soon follow and build a house next door. It was the same in Father's generation—the three brothers and two sisters all bought land near each other on Long Island. Four of the five had houses in Palm Beach, and all five had apartments in New York at One Sutton Place on the East River, and they shared the two camps in Canada.

While I was at Foxcroft, Father bought and did over a stone mill house outside Middleburg, near the Middleburg and Orange County hunts. He also bought and enlarged a shooting box on the land adjoining Ben and Klippy's plantation in Tallahassee. Theirs was a charming house overlooking Jackson Lake, with a garden containing a large collection of camellia bushes. When Klippy and I built ourselves two small wooden houses on Great Island near Hyannis on Cape Cod, the family built a larger house on the same point of land. This is a private island belonging to the Chaces, and the fifth generation of Phippses and the Chaces spend their summer there even now.

Yet these were all satellite homes, and for each of us, Westbury House remained the center, the place where we had grown, the place to which we returned again and again.

*Jay's Orchard Palm Plantation, adjoining Ben's plantation in Tallahassee*

*Aunt Gladys and Grandpoods setting out from Battle Abbey, c. 1906*

# TRAVEL

The last time we used a horse and cart as a practical means of travel and not just for pleasure was on July 4, 1912. That afternoon, Quinn, the head groom, was driving us in the governess' cart when a firecracker went off nearby. The frightened pony bolted, and the carriage fell over, dumping us all onto the grass. No one was hurt, but after that the family turned to cars as its means of transportation. The big black Pierce Arrow would take us to New York via Garden City, Queens, and the Fifty-ninth Street Bridge. It was not a frequent expedition because the journey took a long time and was fraught with difficulties—inevitably a tire would blow out, the engine would develop a problem, or one of the passengers, overcome by the unaccustomed motion, would be sick. Hubert possessed a queasy stomach, so he always got the best seat in front by the window.

To travel on the railroad in those days was a pleasure. The trains were much more comfortable and luxurious than they are now. Quite a few families either owned or rented private cars. We used to rent one each winter to take us to Palm Beach. On arrival, the car would be pulled across the railroad trestle bridge from West Palm Beach and left in a field near the Poincianna Hotel until it was needed to go north at the end of the season.

Our family easily fitted into one car—Mother, Father, the four children, a nurse, and a lady's maid. We also took the dogs and the birds, causing a friend to remark that passing through the Phipps' car was rather like a visit to the zoo. The porters were extremely kind and genial, and the chef would make us stacks of wonderfully fluffy pancakes covered with melted butter and maple syrup.

The rest of the household would come in another private car, and a box car transported the polo ponies. I don't remember these last two conveyances, but others do.

We usually traveled to get to some place and not for the sake of travel. During the warm summer months, when the cases of infantile paralysis became epidemic, everyone who could, would leave the cities and go north into the country. We too would travel north from New York and Long Island. One year, by mistake, our private car was put between the public

*Jay often traveled in the style of his father.*

cars and the diner. Jasha Hamburg, the Austrian violinist and a great pal of Father's, had been put in charge of our journey to Dublin, New Hampshire. He was told not to let anyone into the car under any circumstances. When the hungry and irate passengers came banging at the door, he stood on the other side and exchanged insults and explanations with them. Finally, a conductor arrived and a compromise was reached. We stayed in our compartments behind closed doors while the passengers went through to their lunch, and at the next stop, our car was changed to its proper place at the rear of the train.

*Dita about to embark on a road trip, c. 1906*

My friend Gwendolyn Mackay described a typical overseas trip in the *Old Westbury Gardens News* (Spring, 1977):

It was not uncommon for a family who lived in a house such as Westbury House to travel with twenty or thirty trunks, four or five children, a lady's maid, a valet who could double as a loader if shooting in Scotland was on the agenda, a nurse for the younger children, and a governess for the older ones.

There were many different types of luggage used during these times. Vuitton was a name that was a prerequisite in the baggage collections of the affluent people, as it still is today. There was a square trunk for hats which were placed over convex molds to keep the crowns from crushing and a large trunk for dresses in which the skirts and gowns could be laid flat without folding and layers of white tissue paper protected them from wrinkles. Low, flat steamer trunks, designed especially to go under the bunks in the staterooms, were packed with everything to be worn on ship-board. Evening clothes were always worn for dinner, except on

the last night before landing when the trunks had to be repacked and ready to be taken off the ship first thing in the morning. The gentlemen's silk-hat box, all lined so that the nap of the hat was not rubbed the wrong way, was always part of the collection of luggage as was the leather harness, containing the steamer rugs for wrapping around the ladies and gentlemen as they sat on deck in their steamer chairs. Several shooting sticks were tucked into this harness as a way of carrying them for future use on the moors of Scotland, either by the "guns" waiting in the butts for the grouse to fly over or by the ladies who sometimes joined the men on the moors for lunch. A flat, well-worn leather gun case, probably carrying a matched pair of Purdy guns, and a wicker picnic basket fitted with cutlery, china plates and cups, and sandwich boxes made up the accoutrements of the Scotland-bound traveller. Three fitted cases were for the gentleman and lady, and a tiny case, made by Tiffany to be a replica of the mother's, was for the little girl. In these were carried every silver-topped toilet article that would be needed on the trip, each one engraved with the

*The private car in Southampton Station*

## WHEN THE PHIPPS FAMILY CAME STEAMING HOME ON THE LINER MAURETANIA.

*The Phipps family travels remained legendary. One New York newspaper dubbed the* Mauretania *"The Good Ship Phipps" when it steamed into New York harbor carrying many family members.*

owner's initials. Added to these were a silver inkpot and pen, writing case with blotting paper, corkscrew, folding medicine spoon, a collapsible, silver drinking glass and a knife, fork, and spoon made of ivory. Unbelievable and outmoded as it may seem today, every one of those articles was used constantly on trips at that time.

If England was to be their destination, these travellers would most likely visit relatives or friends either in the country or in London. Perhaps the man would go directly up to Scotland for the salmon fishing or the opening of the grouse season, leaving the ladies in the city for a week or two of shopping and concerts and theater going. They would surely stop in at Rowe and order new sailor suits and hats and coats for their little boys to take home with them to America in September. If they were interested in riding habits and boots, they would order them in London, to be made to their measurements, for there were none better made anywhere in the world.

So for all these varied summer activities an extensive wardrobe was needed for each member of the family to suit every occasion, thus requiring the enormous quantity of trunks and bags that went along on these transatlantic voyages. Unlike today, there were plenty of porters to carry the baggage, and plenty of servants to pack and unpack, to wash, press, and sew, allowing these people of a bygone time to look beautiful and glamorous and always to be so very fashionably and elegantly dressed.

One year, when we were in our teens, the Phipps and Chace families decided that they would take the children abroad to France to acquire some culture and do a little sightseeing. The two families met in Paris. The first evening we went to the Escargot d'Or to eat snails. Mother and I thought the idea was revolting, so we ordered ourselves some chicken hash, which was our usual answer to the exotic menus of foreign

*Dita and Peggie, Paestum, Italy, c. 1926*

restaurants. I suppose that Father and Uncle Martin enjoyed eating escargots, and the others made a gallant attempt to appreciate them too. The snails, which were cooked with garlic and then shoved back into their shells, were covered with a thick red sauce. They were pulled out by means of a small fish fork, but the spiral of the shell and the curly tail of the snail sometimes made this difficult. Poor young Malcolm Chace spilled the sauce all over his shirt front and was horribly embarrassed—so much for food on our first trip to Paris!

The next day, we drove out to Chartres, which was beautiful beyond words. Each of us in his own way was moved by the glory of the rose window and the majesty of the vaulted aisle. We climbed up a tower and looked out over the ancient gray town that encircles the cathedral close—here the worldly and divine reach a complete harmony.

Uncle Malcolm (who was an extrovert), as a typically successful American businessman, was overwhelmed. As we stood under the vast dome of the cathedral, he turned to Father and exclaimed, "Jay, to think that there is something like this in the world, and we stay home every summer and play golf and tennis." I remembered this scene when, many years later, both of them were getting on in years. Uncle Malcolm advised Father, "We have had just about everything that was best in this world, Jay, and we should start seriously making plans for the next one."

Then, of all things to do, we drove to Verdun to visit the First World War trenches where thousands of soldiers, caught by a bombardment, were buried where they stood—their helmets and their bayonets sticking up above the ground. We wandered around the battlefields where Ben found a hand grenade. It didn't seem a good idea for him to carry it, so it was put in the trunk of the car, and we bumped along until we arrived at the town where we were going to spend the night. Ben took the grenade into a jewelry shop to see if they could pull out the pin. The jeweler grabbed it out of Ben's hands, rushed down the street, and threw it into the river.

*Walking among the ruins by the Temple of Hera, Paestum, Italy, c. 1926*

*Nurse Annette and Ben, 1904*

# SERVANTS

The first nurse that I remember was Nurse May. She was trained in England at the Norland School for children's nurses and always wore its uniform, a long brown coat with a velvet collar and a little brown velvet hat perched on top of her hair which was twisted into a bun. Indoors, she wore pale brown dresses, buttoned up the front to a high collar. She was a kindly soul and stayed with us quite a few years. She had been with the Whitney Straights before she came to us, and they were "such good and lovely children." I'm sure that when she left us we too were metamorphosed into a model family. Michael, the youngest, was her pet. She would bring her nanny friends in to see him as he slept, his long dark lashes lying against his rosy cheeks and a little smile parting his lips. He was always able to suppress his laughter until the admiring audience had tiptoed out.

Nurse May was addicted to sayings. As she energetically brushed out my tangled hair and I complained, she would say, "One must suffer to be beautiful," and when the poor little nursery maid carried our tea up four flights of stairs without sugar, Nurse May would say, "Go get it my girl, and in the future, 'let your head save your heels.'"

She looked after Michael and me and kept an eye on Ben. Since Hubert was delicate, he had his own nurse—whom he hated. One evening while the family was at dinner, Ben, in his pajamas, rushed into the dining room saying, "Mother, save me . . . save me. Nurse Udal has spanked Hubert with a hairbrush, and she says if I tell you, she will spank me with the bristle side." Next day, Nurse Udal was gone, and a nice retired trained nurse, Miss Hunter, came to stay with us for the rest of her life.

Mother's protective feeling toward children was again shown when, many years later, the English children stayed with her for the duration of the Second World War. One of the nurses accused her small charge of lying. The little boy stood beside her gazing at his feet and mumbling. Mother said she thought there must have been some mistake, but the nurse replied, "Not at all, and with the parents he has what could you expect but a frightful liar!" Without hesitating, Mother told her, "I would like you to pack and leave tonight. I will pay for a hotel room until the next boat sails for England." The poor woman

*Peggie with her nurse at Dalby House, England, 1906*

didn't at all want to go back to the bombing so she wrote to the British Ambassador, saying that she had been promised a safe job here. Unfortunately for her, one of our English friends was staying at the Embassy at the time, and when the Ambassador asked if anyone knew about this Mrs. Phipps, Margaret Barry said, "I don't know what is in the letter, but anything Mrs. Phipps does is sure to be absolutely right." And that was the end of that.

When I was about seven, I had a governess and moved out of the nursery, where I had first slept with

Ben and then with Michael till I was given a room of my own. The governess' name was Miss Connell, and she was a dear, mousy little thing. I never was so happy. We would go for long walks and read all sorts of beautiful and romantic novels. We were both of a retiring nature, and Mother finally decided that I was becoming too shy, so Miss Connell had to go. I had other governesses after that, but I didn't care for them one way or the other.

At most meals, we sat nine or ten at the table—Father, Mother, Grandpoods, the four of us, a nurse, a governess, and sometimes a tutor. I don't see how Father stood it, but Mother enjoyed it. One of the most exciting events was when older members of the family were out; then the nurses and the governess would have pitched battles, making remarks, and hurling innuendos. To think that grown-up people would fight just the way we did was an eye opener and very satisfactory to us.

When we were really small, we had breakfast and lunch with the family and high tea upstairs in the nursery. Breakfast was not a joy. It consisted of a thick grayish porridge with cream and sugar, an under-cooked egg, some bacon, and a glass of warm milk. In the middle of the morning, we had beef tea. These foods were supposed to be very healthful and maybe they were, but since reaching the age of selection, I have never touched milk, eggs, or red meat.

The other meals were delicious, ordered by Mother with a careful eye to each of our preferences. We were especially fond of chocolate in all forms, chocolate ice cream with fudge and marshmallow sauce, or chocolate layer cake covered with thick cream. Sundays we usually had a roast of beef with the end bits well browned for Mother and me.

The farm provided us with fresh cream, butter, and eggs, and the vegetable garden with asparagus, tiny peas, beans, and carrots, and—best of all—newly picked corn. We also had oranges and grapefruit from the family-owned groves in Florida and salmon packed in snow sent down from our camp in Canada.

I don't think we ever had a French chef or cook. Since we were not allowed in the basement kitchen, I don't remember any specific cook at all. But we certainly enjoyed our meals, which appeared regularly four times a day, and we also enjoyed the company that sat around the table or came to chat at teatime. None of us was more than normally fond of food, but, of course, Mother and I thought about it most because we were always just about to go on a thinning diet.

When we were a bit older, Mother engaged various mademoiselles to teach us French; however, as we knew that Father did not like the French, we were able to get rid of all of them quite easily. As teenagers, the boys had a series of tutors to help them through their examinations.

*Harry Holt, the family chauffeur, in 1906*

*Dita and Nurse Annette outside Battle Abbey, 1904*

Westbury House was always a busy, cheerful place. Besides the family, there were about fourteen servants who lived with us. For the third or children's floor, there were two nurses and a nursery maid. On the second floor, two housemaids and a lady's maid. In the pantry were two footmen and a butler, and downstairs, a cook, kitchen maid, maid for the servants' dining room, an "odd" or handyman, and two laundresses.

Though there were many servants who came to work for the family throughout the years, the ones I remember the best were two of the butlers, the head groom, and the chauffeur. The first butler was called Hendy. He was short and fat, with the pompous air of the perfect butler. One day at lunch, when he was bending over to pass Father a dish of vegetables, Michael slipped from his chair, ran around the table, and gave him a big spank. For a moment there was a horrified silence, and then we all burst out laughing. This act might have been an irresistible temptation or an act of vengeance, for Hendy had always been our archenemy. He constantly accused us of taking sweets from the pantry. In those days, candy was a treat—one chocolate after lunch, if you had eaten all your meat and vegetables. Under these circumstances, therefore, we had no moral qualms about raiding the pantry for anything sweet we could find, preferably marshallow fluff.

During Hendy's years, we had a second footman we called Smiley. That wasn't really his name; it was William Smelley. We already had one footman called William, and one just couldn't say "Smelley, please pass the potatoes," so he became Smiley. I also remember a good-looking young Scottish footman who carried a dirk in his sock. He would show it to us when no one was around.

Our next butler was William Green. Actually his name was Basil Brown, but Basil was not considered an appropriate name for a butler, so he was called William; "Green" just got added on as a mistaken color. He was handsome, agreeable, and charming, looking more like a movie star than a butler. His only drawback was that he didn't believe in alcohol, so at parties he was very slow at passing the drinks to the guests and made a point of never filling family glasses more than halfway up.

All the maids were in love with him—one of them so much so that he had to marry her. This was sad because she was a plain and bossy woman—but later on in life, he married a charming waitress and was very happy. He left us to join the army for the war years, where I believe he had an excellent army career. So Mother had to replace him temporarily with a doddering old English butler whom she hated and was always threatening to fire. I advised her to put up with him, at least for a while, as it was so

*Ben,* right, *and Hubert in a baby-seat known as a governess chair, under the watchful eye of his nurse*

hard to get any servants during the war. Mother answered, "I don't think I can keep him. I hate the way he is always trying to kiss those sweet young pantry maids." I said, "Mother, you loved William and you know he was always kissing the maids. We had to be careful to whistle or sing as we went down the corridor to the pantry door." "Yes, I know," said Mother, "but he kissed them in a nicer way."

Our head groom, Joe Quinn, looked after the hunters and polo ponies and also taught us to ride. He had seven children. The ones near our age were our constant companions, and we would ride together all over the countryside. Once when Hubert fell off

his pony, he swore a blue streak—and then, thinking that perhaps he had gone a bit too far, he lay on the grass and pretended that he had a slight case of concussion. Quinn looked at me in shocked astonishment. "Miss Peggie, where did he ever learn such language?" Being around the stables so much had made the boys very efficient in the art of swearing. Quinn invented Quinn's Liniment for horses and made quite a lot of money out of it, but still he stayed with us until he was too old to work and then retired to the village.

When we were small, Harry Holt, the head chauffeur, was our favorite. All summer long, he drove us daily to Piping Rock beach for a picnic lunch. The best-behaved child had the privilege of sitting beside him in the front seat. Later he drove us to St. Bernard's School in Westbury and gave us turns at steering the Ford Model T. He married a beautiful Irish girl who was nursery maid to our cousins. Uncle Hal told Father, "The children's nursery maid is so pretty I don't dare go near the nursery." Holt stayed with us for over forty years.

Mother had two lady's maids during the fifty years that she lived in Westbury, each of them staying about half of that time. The first was a Frenchwoman, and the second was Scottish with a lovely brogue. They looked after her room and her clothes, and they walked the dogs. When she was ill, they took complete care of her—allowing themselves a certain amount of bossiness when her health was concerned. In contrast to many of the biographies of lady's maids to famous ladies, the relationship between a lady's maid and her mistress was often a very close and affectionate one. The numerous maids that I have known in our families were most devoted. Many, many years ago when I was staying with my cousin in London, her maid, Gibby, asked if I would like her to help me dress. This didn't mean simply doing up the back buttons as I thought, but rather, solemnly holding out each piece of underclothes for me to climb into. I found this embarrassing for both of us, but for Gibby it was just a routine act of helpfulness.

Everyone lives between two or even three eras. For an adult actually to be dressed by a maid seemed to me ridiculous. All the same, thirty years later I was quite surprised when I went out to see my newly married daughter in California; I was met by her housekeeper with hugs and kisses and the genial remark, "Well, I never would have thought that such a lovely, tall young lady would have such a tiny mother—I didn't think you would be like that." Now, of course, it isn't necessary to adjust oneself to the changing manners of domestic servants because there are practically none left. This is a shame. I think if servants were unionized, with set wages and hours as with other jobs, prejudice about working in someone else's house would disappear. A live-in chef gets about as much as a junior company officer, and he doesn't have to spend a cent of his salary on living expenses—the same goes for a housekeeper as opposed to a factory worker.

*Quinn, the head groom at Westbury House for over forty years*

*Peggie, 1914, holding Butterfly, the runt of the beagle pack*

Dogs were a most important part of our family and of the life of Westbury House. Even in early photos, Mother is often shown with a small dog of rather peculiar parentage in her arms, either Impy or Bridget.

Around the time of the First World War and afterwards, there were four dogs in residence. Ben, Hubert, and I all had police dogs—Roswald, Joffre, and Doreen respectively. Mother had a husky. The dogs were thoroughly spoiled. The only discipline was that they were forbidden to come into the dining room, and we were not allowed to boast about them during meals as this led to squabbles. This was well before the time that trained German police dogs became fashionable as watch dogs. The training and in-breeding of these dogs made them nervous, and they were often more apt to attack friends and relatives than to chase away robbers or kidnappers, and so their popularity has waned somewhat. Our dogs were good-natured and caused no trouble. Only once, my Doreen bit Klippy as we were playing tag. I told her that if she ever mentioned it to anyone, I would never invite her to Westbury again. She never told, and for ten years she was our most constant visitor.

Later, Mother and I had long-haired dachshunds. They were dear little dogs, faithful and easy. Mine went with me on my honeymoon with Gordon Douglas. I had no idea of taking her, but Mother insisted that my lady's maid go along with me, and the maid would not leave the dog. I did not like this plan, but it turned out to be quite convenient as we spent most of our time in my mother-in-law's château in Touraine; when we left for England, because of strict English quarantine laws, the dogs went home with the maid. By then it was dogs, plural. We had bought an enormous boxer while we were in Paris. When we went to the kennels to buy a dog, we had no difficulty in making a choice, for a large boxer rushed up to Gordon, almost knocked him down, and covered his face with wet kisses. He came back to Paris sitting in the rumble seat. The French, though they are not really dog lovers like the English, are very sensible about dogs. Max was allowed in all the hotels and restaurants and was always offered either food or water. One restaurant even grew him some grass in a large flower pot. We lost him one afternoon;

*Spike*

and after a frantic search all over Paris, we found him in the Ritz bar. He liked to go around in the revolving door. One of my sillier memories is of taking Maxie with us to a very expensive and over-decorated men's shop. As I waited for Gordon to buy something, I thought, "Imagine, they even have a fountain." They didn't. It was Maxie watering a large potted plant. We

*Jay and Joffie aboard the Sphinx, c. 1928*

*Peggie and Doreen, Westbury House, 1915*

*Hubert and Michael with a goat from the Westbury farm*

quickly left—covered with confusion and desperately trying not to laugh. Max was a wonderful dog, so good-natured with children and formidable as a watch dog. He was with me so much before my daughter Dita was born that Aunt Amy feared the baby might have a pug nose.

One year Ben bought a pit bulldog from an advertisement of fighting dogs and eventually all of us followed suit. Pit bulls are the most intelligent and amusing dogs with one great drawback—they were bred to fight, and ours were constantly having the most horrendous battles. It is illegal to have dog fights or cockfights; nonetheless, many still took place, especially in the Midwest and the South.

Our most famous pet was a pit bull belonging to Michael. Spike is the only dog known to have spent three terms in St. Paul's School. Years later when Michael became a ten-goal polo player, he often had his picture taken with Spike who then became quite well known. One time Spike disappeared for several days. Thinking he must have been run over, we were in despair. Then an anonymous person called Michael on the phone and said, "There is a dog chained up

*Dita giving the dogs an outing on her motor chair, Westbury House, 1950*

*The Westbury dog show, c. 1918:* from left, *Ogden, Peggie, Michael, and Barbara Phipps*

in a yard near us who howls all the time. I think from the pictures I've seen that he looks like yours." Michael drove to the village to the given address, opened the yard gate, unleashed Spike, and took him home.

Spike sired several legitimate and illegitimate families. Such was his reputation that it was never difficult to find homes for his puppies. Unfortunately, Michael gave one to Mother. He was called Monty after General Montgomery, and never was there a more spoiled and disagreeable character. He bit innumerable people, sometimes just a nip, other times, a real bite. As Mother was an older lady and the hostess, often the victims did not complain; if they did, however, they were treated very unsympathetically. Though she was the most kind and understanding person, Mother always took the dog's side.

Concurrent with and after Monty, Mother usually had two or three miniature long-haired dachshunds. They were most attractive, with golden or chocolate colored coats, and were also very greedy and lazy. They would go all over the garden with Mother in her electric chair. It was a pretty sight to see her sitting in her car with the fringe on top, the dogs

surrounding her. If they were pushed off the car for some exercise, they would just sit on the path until they were picked up. Later on when Mother was really old and didn't use her car frequently, the lady's maid Margaret would take the dogs for a walk in a pram. Once a curious motorist having driven up the front drive saw Margaret wheeling her charges in front of the house. They stopped the car in some embarrassment and asked, "Excuse me, but what sort of an establishment is this?" I don't suppose they believed her when she said it was a private home.

Because of their sedentary habits, Teefy, Honey, and Happy were often sent to the vet to get thin. Mother was not amused when Michael, to tease her, said, "You must be Dr. Crawford's favorite customer. You send the dogs to be thinned so he gives them nothing but water and sends them back with a large bill."

We had other pets too. I had an appealing little marmoset for a short while. Ben had a very attractive mongoose named Rikki Tikki Tavi and an equally unattractive bat, a deodorized skunk, and a raccoon. Hubert had racing whippets, weasels, and fighting cocks.

*Ben with Spike,* left, *and Chewie*

*The Westbury dog show, c. 1918:* from left, *Barbara Phipps
and her mother Mrs. Hal Phipps, Ogden Phipps, Peggie, Mrs.
George Kent, Ben, Dita, Michael, Miss Hunter, and Hubert,
showing Foche*

Right, *Michael Phipps in action along the boards*

# POLO

Westbury was pervaded by polo. In our house, the boys never stopped discussing the skills and courage of the respective players and their polo ponies, which is why Mother, Grandpoods, and I sat at one end of the table and spoke about other things. Not that we weren't also interested in the game and enthralled by Michael's rising star and the equally exciting matches played by Ben and Hubert, but horse talk at every meal was a bit too much. Mother and I loved clothes, and we enjoyed talking about them and exchanging a bit of gossip.

Later, when we were young marrieds, my pretty sister-in-law Molly complained sadly to me about the social life of polo wives. For example, she and Michael were invited to a large dinner party after one of the big games. She had bought a new dress for the occasion and spent the afternoon at the hairdressers. In fact, she looked quite ravishing, but to what effect? When the men arrived, they were all in a group at one end of the room; after a few polite words to her, her dinner partners resumed their conversation over her dinner plate; and to top it all, when the men joined the ladies after dinner, there was always a polo player who would insist on going home early to be ready for the next day's game.

Before the First World War, the English team stayed with us for the games. When the games were at the Meadow Brook Club, the family and players would come home for tea, and that's where we came into the picture. My three brothers and I had an arrangement with the team that after the final game we would have a picnic at night on the island in the middle of the lake. Strangely enough, I can't remember the picnic having taken place, but the excitement of stealing food from the tea table, under the very eyes of our parents, and stashing it away for the great event was unforgettable. I used to have a pocket for my handkerchief which I wore on a ribbon around my waist between my dress and my petticoat. This was a good hiding place. Of course, the boys had regular pockets in which to slip a small sandwich or cookie. One of the team, a dashing captain of the Royal Guards, sequestered a whole chocolate cake in a moment when the red drawing room was empty and hid it under the sofa. Unfortunately, it was discovered by one of the dogs who happily licked off all the icing.

*Michael,* left, *with his cousin Winston Guest, both ten-goal players*

It was a time of pomp and gaiety for the grown-ups and of magic and excitement for us. Who won the polo matches was the most important thing in the world, and the charm of our young guests overcame our patriotism as we rooted madly for the English.

A year or two later I received a letter from Captain Cheap, our favorite, describing his life in the trenches and planning new and better picnics. I was very proud of these letters. Then, in the middle of the war, they stopped.

Years later I found an old envelope with some letters and three or four faded snapshots of a dugout, a vague figure standing in the background. It occurred

*Members' stand at the Meadow Brook Club, c. 1934*

to me then that the letters written to a little girl must have been written in the hope that they would be read to her by a pretty and charming young mother who would feel sorry for a lonely young man in the cold and mud of the trenches and would remember him as part of that halcyon summer of 1912.

As everyone in Westbury was involved in polo, I have asked several close friends and neighbors to share their impressions. Mrs. Frederick Prince writes:

> There never was a more glamorous sight than the Number One Polo Field at Meadow Brook on the day of an International Game—the emerald green grass, the blue-painted stands, the length of the field on each side, topped by national flags, and, prior to the game, the parade of the world's finest polo ponies.

People arrived on foot from the parking spaces and the special train from New York. The small center Club House Stand had boxes for families of the players and guests—a total of fifty-thousand people attended. The opposing teams rode to the center of the field, the umpire blew his whistle, threw down the ball, and the game was on.

Brilliant horsemen, clever mallet work, fast ponies, occasional collisions and falls, penalties called—all made for a thrilling spectacle. Between periods, of which there were eight, the spectators could walk to the end of the field to look at the ponies being sponged and rubbed down by grooms, neatly dressed in clean shirts with ties, buff breeches, and polished leather leggings and shoes. When the game was over, later in the evening, the ponies were walked on the dusty roads, home to their respective stables. A groom's wage was eighty-five dollars a month, and he looked after four ponies.

*Jay Phipps and Thomas Hitchcock, Sr.,* left, *spectators at the Meadow Brook Club*

*Dita,* left, *and Mrs. W. R. Grace attending an auction of ponies at Post's Polo Field*

*An international match, c. 1934*

*Action along the boards*

*Michael, c. 1934, hitting an offside forward shot*

Above: from left, *Michael, Wesley White, Harvey Shaffer, Raymond Guest, Stewart Iglehart* (in background), *and Bradley Martin, 1933*
Right: *Michael straightening the mallets before a match*

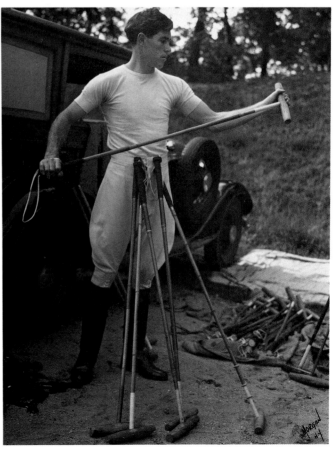

The year before the United States team went to England to bring back the cup, Mrs. Devereux Milburn and Mrs. J. Watson Webb watched each practice game. Each one kept a book on who played what pony, how many periods a pony played, and how it went. The records proved a great help in choosing which ponies were to be taken overseas.

I remember one of my friends gave a ticket to one of the big matches to her hairdresser who, when asked, how she liked the game, replied, "It was *so* exciting, but how do they ever train the ponies to kick the ball?"

Another old friend, Jimmy Mills, remembers polo at Westbury and wrote to me about "the good old days."

In those days, there were two groups of youngsters, like the baby-league baseball kids

*Team meeting at half time, 1934:* from left, *D. Stewart Iglehart, Louis Stoddard, Jimmy Mills, Billy Post, Elbridge T. Gerry, and Michael Phipps*

Above: *At Bostwick field:* from left, *G. W. Bostwick, Gerald Balding, Tommy Hitchcock, Jr., J. H. Whitney, Michael Phipps, Winston Guest, Stewart Iglehart, and Raymond Guest*    Right: *In pursuit*

of today. Mrs. Thomas Hitchcock had one group, known as the Meadow Larks. Among them were Freddy Nicholas, Bobby and Ebby Gerry, Frankie Hitchcock, Cocie Rathborne, Stewart and Philip Iglehart, Bobby Young, Harry Cram, and myself. Our greatest adversaries were the members of the Phipps group who consisted of Bradley and Townsend Martin, Raymond and Winston Guest, and, of course, Michael, Hubert, and Ben Phipps.

These battles were on a very friendly but most serious basis. Our parents would argue our merits. Worried mothers would pinch one another black and blue when a collision was about to occur and their little darlings were sent sprawling to the turf. Fathers had their own complaints. It was criminal to make their sons work, as they were always too tired to play in the evenings. Of course, on Saturdays they were still tired as they had been "tripping the light fantastic" till 4:00 A.M.

Reflecting back half a century, if we only had today such wonderful people, with such great foresight as Mrs. Hitchcock and Jay Phipps, to organize the polo bush leagues, perhaps we could develop a team to go back to Argentina and retrieve the much cherished Cup of the Americas which has been there too long. We brought it back in 1932 but promptly lost it again, and it has stayed in Argentina since.

I am fortunate in my youth to have played the game of polo with all of the greats of the thirties. If I were asked to name an "All-Star American" team, my selection would be as follows: No. 1—Michael G. Phipps; No. 2—Thomas Hitchcock, Jr.; No. 3—Winston F. C. Guest; Back—Devereux Milburn.

Michael Phipps was always beautifully mounted. Brave as a lion, he was the best number one in our lifetime. Tommy Hitchcock was the greatest ever and that includes Harricott of Argentina. He could do things that no other player could do. He was No. 2 on the team that brought the Westchester Cup back from England.

Having played with Winston Guest often, winning the British Open in 1937 and the East-West Series in 1934, I can say that he was a truly fantastic player, and many times, if your team was in trouble, he would always pull the chestnuts out of the fire. He too was always well mounted and a great hitter. Dev Milburn was the first Back to change the character of play of the game. The principal purpose of a Back was to defend; not Dev Milburn—the first Back to attack and attack. But when it came to defending, he was there too, and he had the biggest booming backhand shot imaginable so the boys up front could carry on the attack.

Happily, today polo is becoming popular again and returning to Long Island and even to Westbury House. Following an international match at the Meadow Brook Club in the summer of 1985, the house and the gardens again rang with the laughter and conversation of a gathering of polo enthusiasts, though on this occasion, it was a corporate-sponsored and not a family party.

*The winner's circle, 1938:* center area, from left, *C. V. Whitney, Stewart Iglehart, Mrs. Whitney, C. Smith, and Michael Phipps*

*Peggie Phipps Boegner, Old Westbury Gardens, 1978*

# GARDENS

The idea of preserving the gardens at Westbury grew slowly, one step leading to another. None of us had ever thought about what would happen to the family's place after Father and Mother were gone. Then, luckily, when Father was well over seventy, Ben persuaded him to set up a foundation with the idea in mind that Mother's gardens could be bought and kept in her memory. When Ben told this to Mother she smiled and said, "Yes, of course, dear." It had never occurred to her that her beloved gardens might cease to exist.

It was about this time that she had confided to me her hope that I would eventually live in the house, as she was confident that I wouldn't change anything. Of course, I could not afford to live there, nor did I want to cope with the running of a large house and garden; and yet as things have turned out, her wishes have been fulfilled. The untouched house stands serenely in its gardens just as it did during her lifetime.

In Mother's will, she left the house and land to me and my children, the contents of the house to me alone. I have given the furnishings to "The Gardens," so the house is left intact—nothing added or changed and nothing taken away. However, we did have to sell some land; the polo fields were sold to a real estate developer, but by now the new houses are well planted out and cannot be seen.

Our original plan was to keep the Walled Garden and the Rose Garden in memory of Mother and to sell the rest of the place. Not one of us seemed to want such a large house, but we were sad to think that it would be destroyed. Ben and Michael who looked after Father's foundation had planned to use half of it to establish a park in Florida in his memory, but now, happily, they decided it would be a greater tribute to let the foundation buy the house and seventy acres from my husband Etienne and me and give it to the public. They thought because of the suspicious nature of the I.R.S. the grounds would have to become a public park and the house rented or donated to some established educational or charitable institution. However, one day Bob and Ethel Blum brought Robert Moses over to see the gardens and to give us some advice. As he walked by the West Pond and watched a family of Canada geese proudly parading their goslings, Mr. Moses turned to Etienne

*Margarita Grace Phipps on the terrace steps—the gardens today reflect her vision.*

and said, "Don't offer this to the county or state. It would never be the same. Give it to the public, but have your family and friends run it."

Etienne was intrigued by our conversation with Mr. Moses. We thought that Westbury House and the gardens might be kept safe and whole, very much in the tradition of the stately homes of England, a national treasure to be enjoyed and supported by the public. So Etienne immediately collected some photographs of the house with its long avenues of beech and linden and took them to Washington. There, through the kind office of Edward Burling, of Acheson, Covington and Burling, a law firm we knew well, a meeting with Mr. Ralph Holland, head of the National Trust, was arranged. Mr. Holland had visited Etienne and me at Westbury House and had immensely admired it. With his generous assistance, we became a nonprofit organization for the purpose of preserving the house and gardens for the benefit of the public.

This arrangement was a lucky one for it enabled us to keep the gardens in the peaceful classical tradition of a private country place, and at the same time, both the gardens and the public benefitted by its official standing.

We were taken off the federal, state, and county tax rolls, and the last obstacle to the inauguration of Old Westbury Gardens had been removed. Then, as opening day approached, we suddenly discovered that we had made a rather large blunder. Somehow we had not thought to get permission from the Village of Old Westbury before we opened. These were the officials who were the most involved and might perhaps resent having seventy acres of tax-free land in their midst. The day of the village meeting we rushed from house to house collecting signatures of

residents who were in favor of preserving the gardens. We arrived at the meeting bolstered by a list of a hundred names only to find that no one was there to object. We were given permission to open and soon after received our full complement of permits. It was stipulated that the gardens were to be run by a board of eleven directors: five members of the family and six friends and neighbors. The J. S. Phipps Foundation gave us fifty thousand dollars, and we opened our gates.

At first, we did not show the house, as our income derived from the foundation and the visitor fees was hardly adequate to run the gardens alone. Our main wish was to have the gardens live on, and we imagined a few people wandering around enjoying the flowers and the trees. In my mind, they were mostly

*The opening day ceremony, Old Westbury Gardens, 1959.* From left, front row: *Judy Phipps, Peggie Phipps Boegner, Happy Rockefeller, Etienne Boegner, Dorothy Hutton, Dorothy Leger, and other guests*

*Westbury House—the north facade as seen from the end of the beech allée*

old ladies. We soon found that we needed to augment our entrance fees, so we engaged a publicity agent who advertised us as part of the "Gold Coast of Long Island." This seemed strange to me and my brothers who pictured the place as just a charming country house set in an old-fashioned park.

To become better known, we were advised to have a free day. As the gates opened, the whole of Long Island poured in. The house rocked with the crush of human bodies, and by two o'clock, it could hold no more. I stood at the front door and suggested that the visitors go around the gardens first. Everyone was agreeable except one large (oversized) man who looked at me in disgust and said, "I did not come here to see a garden—I came here to see how the other half lived." This was one of the few times that I remember feeling angry and sad at having our home opened to strangers.

I often have been asked if I didn't mind seeing the public walking around. I really don't. Through the years, most people have been so nice and sensitive to the beauty of the place; and if by chance they recognized me, their thanks have been truly touching. In fact, I have been so fond of the visitors that some days in early October when the tourists have thinned out and the leaves have started to turn orange and gold and the Walled Garden is a mass of bloom, I have walked in the deserted gardens and felt like standing by the gates and calling to the passing cars, "Please come in—you don't have to pay. I can't bear to see all this loveliness go unseen."

Through the years, we acquired committee members and volunteers. We started a yearly membership drive; we opened a few rooms on the ground floor and later included the second floor bedrooms. All this was costing more and more money, and every year there would be a deficit. Finally, Ben and Michael, abandoning their hopes of having Father's

*Westbury House today—the south facade and terrace, viewed from the South Lawn.*

Following page: *The dining room, designed by George Crawley for the Fifth Avenue home of Harry and Annie Phipps, was installed in a new wing of Westbury House in 1927 following the demolition of the New York townhouse.*

*The water lily pool in the Walled Garden*

*The terrace staircase leading to the South Lawn*

foundation support both Westbury and a wildlife park in the Florida Everglades, gave the whole foundation to the Gardens.

As I write this, the Gardens are eighty years old and have been open to the public for twenty-six years. Many of the first group of directors are gone, and younger workers have taken their places, but the feeling that inspired us all is still there—the feeling that we were entrusted with something of beauty that we must nurture and protect.

Currently, there are many new sides to the Gardens. We found that the pictures and the furniture in the house not only mirrored the taste of the early nineteenth century but also constituted a unique and very valuable collection of eighteenth-century furniture and paintings whose worth escalates every year. So, Westbury House is becoming a museum, though this title will in no way change its atmosphere of being a family house.

In the Gardens, there are now horticultural classes, and "events" are held on the front lawn: pop concerts, pageants, and old car rallies. We invite groups and institutions to visit us, and on Sundays the Gardens are as crowded with visitors as a city park. All of this gives pleasure and instruction to many people and helps us with the upkeep.

Still, our main object has been to preserve the charm and beauty of the Gardens in the tradition of my parents during their long and happy time and sometimes to give a sense of delight and beauty to the gentle, welcome visitors.

Above: *A panoramic overview of the Walled Garden*
Right: *Peggie Phipps' thatch-cottage playhouse*

*Westbury House, the east side, seen from the lake*

Overleaf: *After the ball*

# Photocredits

Many of the photographs in this book were taken by family members. Of those by others, particularly the professional photographers of the last century, we were able to identify many but not all from their signatures or photo stamps. They are listed here alphabetically, their work identified by page number and location.

Arony (New York): 111. L. Alman (New York): 73, left; 112, bottom; 172; 182, top; 189, bottom left. Bachrach: 75. J. Ballantine: 32–33. Curtis Bell: 114–15; 128; 161; 206. J. H. Blomfield (Royal Studios, Hastings, England): 185, top. Bradley (New York): 132, 138; 160. Bullingham (London): 113. J. Burton & Sons (Leicester, England): 102; 142, bottom. Campbell & Gray: 179; 236. Richard Cheek: 96, top; 208–209; 270–71; 274; 276. C. C. Cook (New York): 203, bottom. Courret: 173. B. L. Dabbs (Pittsburgh): 13; 15; 17; 24, bottom; 26, top right, bottom left, and bottom right; 27; 50; 57. Dana (New York): 31. Thomas Neil Darling: 235, bottom. Luke C. Dillon (Washington, D.C.): 34, bottom right. Thomas Falls: 188. Frank H. Foltz (Bedford, Pennsylvania): 29, top. Freudy: 77; 166, bottom; 216–17; 212–13; 256; 257; 258; 259, top left; 260; 261; 263; 264; 265. R. Garzón (Granada, Spain): 36; 37. Gerschel (Paris): 189, top left. F. E. Ginsberg (New York): 226; 227; 229. Gottscho-Schleisner: 94–95; 272–73. Gutekunst (Philadelphia): 22. Heawood, Leicester & Melton: 182–83. M.E. Hewitt Studio: 68; 69; 228. Ira L. Hill (New York): 154. Histed: 52; 65. Horst: 155, top. Karanjian: 118. Keystone View Co. (New York): 259, top right. Koehne (Palm Beach): frontispiece; 147; 148; 149; 204–205. W. Kurtz: 24, top. G. Lekegian & Co. (Cairo, Egypt): 195. Pirie MacDonald (New York): 100. Macnabb (New York): 14, top. Marshall & Green (New York): 116; 156. McClellan Photo (West Palm Beach): 235, top. Mendelssohn (London): 8; 110; 186; 191. Metcalfe (Palm Beach): 218. Moffett: 181, bottom. Morgan: 214; 262, top. National (New York): 136, top; 253. *The New York Times:* 157, bottom. R. Newell & Son: 12. Pach Brothers (New York): 58, bottom; 123; 162. William Pickering: 92–93. The Pictorial News Co.: 146, top. B. Frank Puffer (New York and Palm Beach): 146, bottom. Purviance's Photographic Rooms (Pittsburgh): 14, bottom. Erwin Raupp (Dresden): 47. M. Rice (Bridgetown, Nova Scotia): 34, bottom right. A. Ross (Stonehaven and Laurencekirk, England): 72. Neil Rothman: 97. Rotofotos (New York): 165. Russell: 46. Mike Sirico: 108, right. W. L. H. Skeen (Ceylon): 30. Ken Spencer: 266. Captain James Suydam (New York): 78. Swain (London): 129. Taber (San Francisco): 25, bottom. K. Tamamura (Yokohama, Japan): 67. J. Thomson (London): 49; 59. Frank Turgeon, Jr. (Palm Beach): 167. Underwood & Underwood: 252. Franz Volker (Austria): 35, top right. Waléry (Nice): 26, top left; 29, bottom. J. Weston & Son (London): false title page; opposite contents page; 133; 135; 139; 140; 174–75; 242; 243. White: 98; 151; 163, right. Wilhelm: 190. Wurts Brothers Photo: 70–71.